onions and cucumbers and plums

# onions and cucumbers and plums

*Granger Index Reprint Series*

**BOOKS FOR LIBRARIES PRESS**
FREEPORT, NEW YORK

# 46

## YIDDISH
## POEMS
### in english

Sarah Zweig Betsky

Grateful acknowledgment is made to the
Morris and Emma Schaver Publication Fund
for Jewish Studies for financial assistance
in making possible the publication of this
volume.

(Acknowledgment to original edition)

STANDARD BOOK NUMBER:
8369-6002-5

LIBRARY OF CONGRESS CATALOG CARD NUMBER:
70-76932

MANUFACTURED
BY
HALLMARK LITHOGRAPHERS, INC.
IN THE U.S.A.

for my mother, Celia Dokser Zweig

and for my father, Abraham

who gave me this book

# PREFACE

Many debts must be acknowledged here, and many more must remain implicit in old friendships and influences. I must thank Wayne State University and its Department of English, the first in this country to award a degree based on research into Yiddish studies. Dr. Harold A. Basilius of Wayne should be held responsible for urging this book from start to finish, and its very completion is a tribute to his distinguished teaching ability. The poets themselves, or their executors, have kindly permitted the inclusion of their poems. The Wayne English Department has granted me permission to include two translations which they have published in *Wayne Writers,* number 1, fall, 1956. Many eyes have helped in the tedious work of emendation and correction: Isaac Franck, A. M. Klein, S. Maltz, John E. Moore, Bernard Heringman, Dorothy McKinnon Brown and Bernard Goldman. There is a great debt also to the Yiddish schools (in my case, the Arbeiter Ring Shulen of Detroit), which helped several generations of American-born Jews share in the culture which might otherwise have been denied them. Of my Yiddish teachers, the late Chaim Raden was responsible for my first interest in Yiddish poetry, and his premature death prevented me from thanking him as an adult for that which he gave freely and lovingly to a child. That Seymour Betsky has been my most affectionate and critical friend he knows by my dependence on his intelligence at all times. My father's stubborn and sensitive insistence on my special kind of education is equally at fault. This is his book, really, just as it is my mother's, both of whose vanished beauty only the tenderness of Yiddish can describe.

My thanks are also due to Miss Janet Olender, the librarian of Congregation Shaarey-Zedek, Detroit, and to Samuel Sigal, City Editor, *Jewish Daily Forward,* for assistance in collecting and typing out authentic Yiddish texts, and to Charles E. Feinberg, for permitting me to have drawings made of his collection of Torah pointers (*yad*) for the illustrations.

S. Z. B.

# CONTENTS

## o my world of a thousand colors                3

## onions and cucumbers and plums                47

# how blessed am I and how blessed and blessed                                   85

# children still die of fear                                     153

# I burn and I burn and I am not consumed

# INTRODUCTION

"How lucky I am — I'm an orphan!" These are the words Mottel, the young boy of Sholem Aleichem's novel, *Mottel the Cantor's Son*, shouts when his father dies. Mottel loved his father. But think of the advantages of being orphaned in a small town, where everyone knows everyone else, where each man's trouble or joy affects all of them. Mottel is now treated with gentle sadness by the neighbors who once cursed him for stealing apples. He is given delicacies to eat; he is the center of worried discussions about his future. He is elevated from his cheerful naughty-boy role to that of hero. "How lucky I am — I'm an orphan!"

The Yiddish poet introduced to an English speaking world is a Mottel. Like Mottel, he has been living for a long time in self-sufficient joy (and misery) and, like Mottel, must appear orphaned to a world which is unaware of his hidden history, cognizant only of his altered state. Mottel the Yiddish poet comes in these poems dressed in translation-clothes, seeking definition in the larger family of poets.

How shall we describe the Yiddish poet, how name him so that we can understand and judge his works? His history is as old as that of the Yiddish language — a thousand years old — and his prototype and consciousness are even older, as old as the Old Testament. Here are forty-six of the poems written by the Yiddish poet in the twentieth century, and if we wish to consider their adoption through translation into English, we must try to find some homogeneity in their appearance. The problem is difficult. These Yiddish poets share, at first glance, only three characteristics. They all wrote during the last fifty years, and they all used the same language. The third is more complex: each of the poets received a training, inherited from the centuries, in Hebrew and in the Jewish religion.

If we try to name other biographical similarities we are lost. The poets have lived in all parts of the world; were born in one place, educated in another, wrote in still a third. They read as much Byron and Goethe and Eliot and Valéry as they did Solomon or Yehuda Halevi. Some of them have been politically active, some are practising journalists, others are avowed agnostics. Perhaps the poems themselves will offer a unity of interest that will cancel out the disparate quality of the poets' backgrounds.

These poems are concerned with, roughly, the topics of the natural landscape, love for one's family, loneliness, war and destruction, oppression, hope for the future, life in the village or city. Certainly ordinary enough subjects for contemporary poetry, and we mark only the poetry of sensual love missing from the list. The topics of Yiddish poetry will, then, not help us clearly enough in the search for the special qualities of that poetry.

We know poems are formed in characteristic modes and conventions, by different groups of poets, at different times. When we examine Yiddish poetry for these characteristic articulations, we begin to come closer to what Mottel is really like before he becomes translated. We find rhyme and rhythm often self-consciously monotonous and restricted; the simile the most heavily employed figure of speech. The visual form of the poem on the page fluctuates between the rigid and the flexible. The diction is simple, direct, lucid, and the imagery, like the subject matter listed, is obvious, visible. When we are told that these poems, or others like them, have been set to music and then sung as if they were anonymous gifts to the singers, then our poet begins to look more familiar. The Yiddish poet belongs to the world of folk song and street ballad, to the audience which expects and accepts the poem appropriate to the occasion, to the mood, to the needs of its daily life.

The Yiddish poet builds his repertoire of rhetoric and techniques on the tacit traditional modes. Now we can see where his basic training in the Old Testament supports him. Words are to be chanted, as is the liturgy in Hebrew. Immense variation in the chanting, and in the words, is permissible, but these variations will rest ultimately on the same base the people who made the first ones used. Mottel belongs, by language, by training, by his very acceptance of his own orphaned state when it happens, to the people who will never question his eligibility, who take him into their homes.

But we, the adopters, begin to see it is not as simple as that. Given the magnificent inheritance of the Yiddish poets (the cadence of the Biblical line; the story of an ancient people and its survival; the folk art's flexible yet constricting demands) and a tradition from which to draw, surely the characteristics we have noted in subject matter and in manner must lead into a third problem. Do Yiddish poets have special attitudes, revealed by their poems, that make those poems particular creations of a particular history? There are special attitudes. This is a poem written by Itzik Manger, born in what was Roumania and now living in the United States, educated in Berlin, escaped to London during the Hitler era.

The "Lovers of Israel" in the Belsen Death Camp

Reb Moyshe Leyb of Sosov points at the heaps of ash
(the hurricane has just now blown),
his beard shakes, bitterness in every bone:
"Here — take and see, O God, taste and relish."

Reb Wolf of Zbarazh murmurs: "Hear, gentlemen, my sound."
(His voice is an evening-violin dejected.)
"The One above left His vineyard unprotected.
The proof: these heaps of nothing on the ground."

Reb Mayerl from Premishlan leans on his ancient stick,
stands and waits, fevered and heartsick:
"Gentlemen, let us all together now loudly call:

" 'Creator of all worlds, You are strong, dreadful, and great,
but we, the Galicians, for eternity obliterate
Your name from the assembly of True Lovers of Israel.' "

The attitudes, bitterness, anger, sorrow, and best of all, humorous
wryness (the old men against history, the old men against God, the
old men against their own deepest beliefs, the old men and their
beautiful pride) are immediately apparent. On what do such atti-
tudes, in this poem, most clearly rest? God and God's word have
been the only unshakeable possession of the Jew for millennia. Like
all inherited and painfully cherished possessions, God and his word
can be regularly rejected, complained about, scoffed at. The figure
of George Herbert, the seventeenth century British poet, rises to be
set against the Yiddish poet. Both, secure in their possessions, can
afford to examine their contracts, contrive law suits against the bur-
den they bear. But there is an added family nastiness ("Come, roll in
Your mouth the taste of these monstrous sacrifices, these delicacies.")
that only a Yiddish poet can achieve. Along with the intimacy in
one's relation to God (such intimacy that the denial of God in a
Yiddish poem must be taken as literal, just as the son will *not* return
home after the quarrel), goes the troubled intimacy with one's group,
other groups, and one's self. The men of Galicia are your brothers,
but your feelings are not always fraternal towards them.

As Yiddish poet, you may prefer other group activities than dying
in the name of a historical pride. Instead, your intimacy with other
groups in other cultures may be deep and real, but the Patriarchs
beat you with their crooked sticks, and your identity and allegiance
split under their blows. Chaim Grade, a Polish poet recently settled
in America, has tried several times to write the same poem, "The
Song of the Generations." In it, in all the versions, he pictures him-
self asleep, and visited by his father, grandfather, great-grandfather.
Each represents a different phase of European civilization. His great-
grandfather had to suffer religious persecution with unyielding faith,
his grandfather fought under Napoleon to free mankind, his father
met excommunication in his own home and church for his study of
Spinoza and Mendelssohn. All three of them berate Grade, and in a
last attempt to quiet them, he tells them that "we have won," that

there is no longer an enemy of any kind, that the Jew has fought back, conquered, and now belongs with the strong. His father senses the lie first, and the poems end with Grade forced into childhood, cowering under the sheets, as his father beats him. The refrain from all the generations is still, "This is not what we meant, this is not it."

So too your intimacy with yourself is fragmented. You must hold the stance of irony, of self-condemnation, of self-pity, of loneliness carefully poised, or no one will believe, least of all yourself, that you are lucky to be an orphan.

This then is the outstanding characteristic of the Yiddish poem, in form, in content, in attitude: a precarious balance. Everything we have noticed is a means of achieving that balance. There are the conventional modes of folk song, folk legend, and the Old Testament rhythms to help make communication to a scattered and divided audience easier, more valid. There is a shared awareness of a multiple life to use for subject matter, in Babylon, in Russia, in Illinois, a forest, a sob, a river, a child, a musical instrument. There have been so many countries, there is no longer any need for maps — any hill is all hills, the simile drawn from the hill is all similes. There is a shared awareness of a tortuous history and of the word that first began it and the word that always recorded it, and the awareness of a God inseparable from the history or the word. So for believer and non-believer, right into our day, there is a shared and inherited God to be used even when He has been scientifically discarded. He is the vocabulary of the Jew, in or out of the synagogue. He is the self, shaped by the centuries, dualistic, ambivalent, evanescent as physical love (one of the reasons for the non-importance of love poetry: hills and women are so ageless and evanescent), eternal as the bitter hope that He has not remained in a sandy past, but perhaps watches today.

Balance requires objectivity, and the classroom patiently tries to convince us that a knowledge of history bolsters objectivity. What is often overlooked in calling Jews the people of the Book is that the Old Testament is not only a document of a religious revelation but a history book. Here is the log of Jewish life, with entries added by commentators, scholars, poets, through the ages. The Yiddish poet works then with the help of his history, learning from it a sad sense of inevitability (he has seen it all before); learning a refusal, like the Prophets, to make peace with the inevitable "things as they are"; and the most outrageous lesson of all, hope. The tone of the Yiddish poem, the cry of Mottel, balances therefore between passion and coolness.

The poems are occasional verse in a way most English poems no longer are. Yiddish poets write for the daily newspapers, some of them publish a poem a week. If a friend dies, you write a poem for him. If there is an event of great political importance, you write a poem about it. If a child has a birthday or it is the anniversary of an artist's death, you write a poem. Even if you read a new book, or reread an old one, you write a poem about it. This special delight in versifying, a diminishing one surely in our day, has its double-edge. On the one hand, there is an involvement, a sense of connection with the daily world, for each poet; on the other hand, many of these "occasional" poems are poor poems, and Yiddish poets have too often lost their own critical sense, write too much, publish too casually.

Perhaps the most important aspect of the folk song influence on Yiddish poetry is the one that strikes the reader unaccustomed to it. Yiddish poetry is in many ways constructed of reiterated clichés. The rhyme schemes may on occasion appear limited to "blue-you." The sing-song rhythms can be uneven and often unpolished. Punctuation is rarely used as a tool for emphasizing meaning and form. Form itself is loose, casual. These are not accusations of incompetence or laziness; the Yiddish poet works in an idiom of expression that needs flexibility of thought and merely an acceptable form (in the text-book sense) to make a poem. The problem of translation is compounded by this attitude. To give to Yiddish poems a greater range of technical devices than they truly use is a major temptation. That temptation has been avoided by offering a parallel text translation. The original poem is transliterated into Roman letters, and the translation attempts to copy, rather than to recreate, that original. Most translations, of course, are re-writings. This one tries not to be. Often meter and rhyme are sacrificed for the sake of exact meaning. No poem can remain the same in translation. A poem is language, the language of its first writing. Therefore there is no pretence made here of equaling the original, only an attempt to offer in fairly colloquial English an approximation of the original.

The basis for selection of the Yiddish poems is equally simple. Poems were included if they appeared to be good poems, in the sense that image, tone, language, phases of an idea, moved in coherence. Because translation, at best, is not an easy task, or the results usually completely palatable, a further criterion of expediency had to be adopted. If the poem was too specially Yiddish, if its very rhythm and impact had to be footnoted, or even if its vocabulary were specialized and exotic, then it was not included. Such a criterion excluded some of the finest poems, which lost their savor in the process of translation.

Although the final selection emerged, surprisingly, as a moderately representative one, this was not the intention. Many good poets have been slighted — their names would make a solid paragraph — and many living poets have been excluded for no other reason than the exigencies of translation and choice. There are other, and more important, conscious oversights in the selection. The older generations of Yiddish poets have been entirely omitted. First, the work of Bialik, Reisen, Peretz, Yehoash, and others, has been excluded because it calls for a separate volume and separate treatment. Second, their poetry has been more readily available to the English reader than the verse printed here.* I am aware that these omissions are striking to any student of Yiddish literature, and I can only repeat that the present selection seemed most suitable, given the interests of this study.

Another large gap in the selection concerns the poets of social consciousness (Morris Rosenfeld, Bovshover, Edelstadt, etc.). Since the 1880's there has been a large and emotionally fervent group of revolutionary and protest poems, particularly from the immigrant poets in America and from Russia and Poland. However stirring their calls to action and their pictures of poverty and injustice, their verses today sound strained and painful and are too dependent on an act of sympathy beyond the scope of a poem.

If this were a historical study, then, all the generations of Yiddish poets would be included, and all the types of poems represented. It is not such a study, nor does it pretend to critical equity. The poems that would honestly represent the balanced poise of Yiddish poetry at its best, in a language other than the one in which they were written, were the ones chosen. I apologize not to the poets but to the poems I have loved and learned from, since childhood, and have not included here.

A brief summary of Yiddish as a language might help in reading the poems. Jews themselves are notably defensive about its status, even about its aesthetic merits. For many Jews it is the tongue spoken by the new immigrant; the defensiveness is easily explained. The decrying of the merits of Yiddish as a language is another matter. It would seem that some people search for a hierarchy in languages just as they do in painting. Surely the proof of a language is in its creative expressions, and Yiddish culture owns shelves of novels, belles lettres, poetry, and history, that even in translation speak for a remarkable achievement. The tragic side of what might seem a private ethnic civil war is that Jews no longer have to apologize, explain, or quarrel over Yiddish. Yiddish lies in an unmarked grave, along with seven million mouths that gave it voice. It is probably

* Joseph Leftwich, ed., *The Golden Peacock*, Cambridge: Science-Art Publishers, 1939. This is a historical anthology of Yiddish poetry.

the major example of the literal and violent death of a language and of the culture it birthed. Nor has the State of Israel resurrected the corpse. Long ago, Hebrew won the battle against Yiddish as the language most appropriate to a new nation, and so it has come to be. Yiddish is for too many Jews associated with the Ghetto, alienation, poverty, and Middle Europe. Although it is still spoken by many Jews all over the world, the average age of its speakers mitigates against its long continuance. If this picture is wrong, then let the poems stand as an epitaph for a culture almost extinguished, and a hope that it may flow — as cultures have the ability to do — into something equally rich and strong and vital.

The Yiddish language arose approximately a thousand years ago. The oldest dated Yiddish text, 1396, was found in Cologne, but there are others, undated, that are probably older. Yiddish should be dated from the time Jews settled in German countries. The first references to Jews in Germany are in 321 A.D. and 331 A.D., and then there is a gap in recorded materials until the eleventh century. On the basis of these dates and the early dated manuscripts, the history of Yiddish has been traced from the year 1000. Max Weinreich divided this history into the following phases:

| | |
|---|---|
| Beginning (or Genesis) Yiddish | c. 1000 to 1250 |
| Old Yiddish | 1250 to 1500 |
| Middle Yiddish | 1500 to 1700 |
| New Yiddish | 1700 to present |

Jews brought with them a double language heritage to Germany. First, they had their "Hebraisms," the religious vocabulary of Hebrew-Aramaic. Second, they carried into German lands the Romance elements of language they had assimilated in Italy and Gaul. Germany and France were, of course, still one country, and when Jews wandered from France into Germany they usually settled in cities on the Rhine, close to France. Yiddish was born, for calendar purposes, in 1000, near the end of the Old High German period, on the river Rhine between Cologne and the Alsace; and Old Yiddish developed simultaneously with Middle High German. After this parallel growth was completed, Yiddish dropped any dependency on the scheme of German philological history.

Yiddish was long called Judeo-German. It is a German dialect derived, like Modern German, from Middle High German, with the addition of Hebraic elements, and it is written in Hebrew characters. Jewish immigration to Poland in the twelfth century introduced Yiddish into the Slav countries, where it absorbed Slav elements and spread, eventually developing into the language of the Jews of those countries. Similar fructification in two directions continued through the centuries. The peregrinations of the Jews over the globe brought them into contact with many languages and these were assimilated in normal linguistic growth. Today standard literary Yiddish remains the same everywhere. Yiddish is spoken now principally in Europe (where there are still Jewish communities), North and South America, Great Britain, South Africa, and Australia, as well as in scattered communities in every country of the world. Melech Ravitch, vagabond Yiddish writer, maintains that he has never visited a city from Shanghai to Buenos Aires where he has not found a fellow Jew speaking Yiddish. That Yiddish was and to a great extent still is a most important chain binding together a scattered and for centuries landless people there can be little question. That chain was made even stronger by what S. Niger, the Yiddish critic, has called *tsveyshprakhikayt;* bilingualism is an accepted phenomenon. For hundreds of years most Jews, and certainly their writers, were equally at home in Hebrew and Yiddish. Every poet in this selection, for instance, received some kind of Hebrew education and knew Yiddish from the home and the street. Many of them have published in both languages. It is also apparent that the bilingualism had to proliferate into treble, quadruple, linguistic knowledge. French, German, Russian, Polish, and English: at least two of these (and their literatures as well) would be added to the Jew's taken-for-granted language store. This linguistic knowledgeability, necessary for existence in most cases, makes the simplicity, directness, and lack of pedantry in these poems most remarkable.

The poems translated here are the result of what happened to Yiddish writing at the end of the nineteenth century. A rebirth in Yiddish letters occurred then, and the poems in this selection owe their chronological unity to that event. The Age of Enlightenment came late for European Jews, in the early 1800's when civil freedom was partially won, and it called to the artist to leave the Ghetto and join a world from which he had been excluded. But the late nineteenth century was an era of pogroms and anti-Semitism, in eastern Europe especially, and the artist retreated again to his Ghetto to sing folk songs in his mother's tongue. It is there that the roots of twentieth century Yiddish poetry lie. It is ironical that Jewish creativeness seems to bloom in a time of catastrophe, when the individual Jew must reexamine his position among his fellow men. The distrust and deep yearning for the culture of the "others" is evident in many of the poems here.

Just as British and American poetry found at the turn of our century both within itself and in the poetry of the Continent the springs of a new expressiveness, a new colloquial mode, a greater experimentalism, so Yiddish poetry between 1900 and 1914 reflected this new self-consciousness. The poems translated here all mirror this growing up and away from folk art monotone and purely propagandistic or didactic impulses. Yiddish poetry now shares the colors of the cultures in which it is written, and Baudelaire, Rilke, Eliot, and Pound, for example, influence Yiddish poetry as it reshapes its traditional forms.

The poems have been grouped under five headings. A shared content or compulsion has set the tone of each section, but in the recalcitrant manner of art, the individual poems have a tendency to fit equally well under several headings. This inability to rest classified speaks well for the poems.

Here then are forty-six poems, written in the twentieth century by Jewish poets in a thousand-year-old language. Both poems and language are witnesses to an intense cultural creativity, to dependence on the creativity of other peoples, and to awareness of a history and its continued transfiguration into life in the concrete image of the written word. The poem and the language have recorded time past and time lamed in the present. The hope for the future is tinged by wryness, sorrow, intelligence: the earmarks of the Yiddish poem. Mottel's cry echoes passionately in each Yiddish poem, "How lucky I am — I'm an orphan!"

The transliteration key is used consistently in the poetry except when a Yiddish or Hebrew word has appeared so often in an accepted English spelling, that its correct pronunciation is assured (*Chaim,* for example, according to this key would be *Khayem;* or *Einhorn* would be *Aynhorn*). Whenever such a word is used in an English sentence, or is a proper name, the traditional spelling is retained. When the familiar word is part of a Yiddish line or title, the word is spelled according to this key (*Yiddish,* therefore, is spelled *Yidish* in such places).

Apparent discrepancies in the transliteration are caused by the various Yiddish dialects employed for certain words (*zaynen* and *zenen,* both meaning "are," for example). The poets here are usually working in the literary dialect, the Lithuanian in a modified form, but there is a great deal of laxity permitted in the correct usage of certain words. Hebrew, or more accurately Hebraisms, is transliterated according to its Yiddish pronunciation.

This key was generously prepared for me by the YIVO, the Yiddish Scientific Institute. The Institute is the present authority on Yiddish linguistics, and the only debatable point in its key might lie in using the single letter *i* both for the long and short vowel sound *i*.

# TRANSLITERATION KEY
## For Yiddish into Roman Letters

| TRANSLITERATION SYMBOLS | YIDDISH | ENGLISH PRONUNCIATION |
|---|---|---|
| *a* | א, אנדערש | a, father |
| *o* | אָ, גאָט | French: *homme* |
| *v* | ב, מקרב ; וו, ווען | v, valve |
| *g* | ג, גאָר | g, get |
| *d* | ד, דאָס | d, deed |
| *h* | ה, האָבן | h, have |
| *u* | ו, קומען, וואו | u, pull |
| *oy* | וי, קוימען | oy, oyster |
| *z* | ז, אזוי | z, zones |
| *kh* | ח, חוץ ; כ, ך ; כאַפן, בוך | |
| *t* | ט, טאַנץ ; ת, תוך | t, toot |
| *i* | י (vowel), מיש, רויק | i, sit |
| *y* | י (consonant), יאָר, ייד | y, you |
| *ey* | יי, גיין | a, cave |
| *ay* | יי, גלייך | i, ice |
| *k* | כּ, כּלה ; ק, קולטור | k, cook |
| *l* | ל, ליבע | l, lull |
| *m* | מ, ם, מענטש, קום | m, maim |
| *n* | נ, נעכטן | n, noon |
| *s* | ס, סמך ; שׂ, שׂרה ; ת, טעות | s, cease |
| *e* | ע, עסן | e, set |
| *p* | פּ, פּוילן | p, peep |
| *f* | פ, ף, פאַקט, לויף | f, fife |
| *ts* | צ, ץ, צוריק, זאַץ | |
| *r* | ר, רעוואָלוציע | r, rear |
| *sh* | ש, שיין | sh, shut |

(*e* is always a short vowel and is always pronounced.)

onions and cucumbers and plums

O MY WORLD OF A THOUSAND COLORS

These poems celebrate, with variations, the multi-faceted world of the poet. Their tone is generally soft and muted, although there is a rising into a glad exclamation in the river and mowing poems of Moyshe Kulbak. Here we meet his family, as it figures in one of his poem-cycles: the sixteen uncles and their lusty father. We meet also some of the most virile, fresh Yiddish of our day. Kulbak, killed in a Soviet camp sometime in the thirties, gives an explicit picture of the peasant life of the Jew in eastern Europe, a life more indirectly drawn by Abraham Sutskever, one of the younger Yiddish poets, a Partisan fighter in World War II. The late Zisha Landau and Reuben Iceland are lyrical, but sad. Landau was a sensitive and skillful member of the *Yunge* (the Young), an American group who experimented with personalized, impressionistic subjects and forms. Kadie Molodowsky has, perhaps, the clearest lyrical skill of any of her contemporaries, as well as an originality that sets her above other Yiddish women poets. Aaron Zeitlin is generally a "difficult" poet, and his metaphysical verses are reminiscent of concurrent trends in other literatures. David Einhorn has proved himself one of the few selective poets in Yiddish. He has matured slowly and well, evolving through two world wars and several exiles a quiet, sober poetry of tenderness and controlled anger. "In Soft Moss, Muted Steps" is an excellent example of the Yiddish love poem, if it can be called that. The Friday night ritual of candle-lighting is woven into Einhorn's love for a woman, and the Sabbath made a seven day long festival of hushed passion.

# אויף מיין וואנדערפייפל

א בארוועסער וואנדראוניק אויף א שטיין
אין אוונטגאלד,
ווארפט פון זיך אראפ דעם שטויב פון וועלט.
פון וואלד ארוים
דערלאנגט א פלי א פויגל
און טוט א כאפ דאס לעצטע שטיקל זון.

א ווערבע פאזע טייך איז אויך פאראן.

א וועג.
א פעלד.
א צאפלדיקע לאנקע.
געהיימע טריט
פון הונגעריקע וואלקנס.
וואו זענען די הענט, וואס שאפן וואונדער?


## OYF MAYN VANDERFAYFL

A borveser vandrovnik oyf a shteyn
in ovntgold,
varft fun zikh arop dem shtoyb fun velt.
Fun vald aroys
derlangt a fli a foygl
un tut a khap dos letste shtikl zun.

A verbe paze taykh iz oykh faran.

A veg.
A feld.
A tsapldike lonke.
Geheyme trit
fun hungerike volkns.
Vu zenen di hent, vos shafn vunder?

# 1

# ABRAHAM SUTSKEVER

## ON MY WANDER FLUTE

A barefoot vagabond on a stone
in evening gold
casts from himself the world's dust.
Out of the woods
flits a bird in flight,
and snatches the last fragment of sun.

Here is a willow near the river.

A road.
A field.
A quivering meadow.
Muffled footsteps
of hungering clouds.
Where are the hands that shape this wonder?

א לעבעדיקע פֿידל איז אויך פֿאַראַן.

איז וואָס־זשע בלײַבט צו טאָן אין אָט דער שעה,
אָ, וועלט מײַנע אין טויזנט פֿאַרבן! —
סײַדן,
צונויפֿקלײַבן אין טאָרבע פֿונעם ווינט
די רויטע שיינקייט
און ברענגען עס אַהיים אויף אָוונטברויט.

און עלנט ווי אַ באַרג איז אויך פֿאַראַן.

*A lebedike fidl iz oykh faran.*

*Iz vos-zhe blaybt tsu ton in ot der sho,*
*o, velt mayne in toyznt farbn! —*
*Saydn,*
*tsunoyfklaybn in torbe funem vint*
*di royte sheynkayt*
*un brengen es aheym oyf ovnbroyt.*

*Un elnt vi a barg iz oykh faran.*

**1**

Here is a lively fiddle.

What then is left to do in such an hour,
O, my world of a thousand colors,
except
to gather into the knapsack of the wind
the red loveliness
and bring it home for evening bread.

Here is loneliness like a hill.

## ווען ס'בליאַקעװעט מיין אויג

ווען ס'בליאַקעװעט מיין אויג,
איז גוט, װאָס ס'בלייבט דער הימל בלוי,
און ס'איז דער װאַלד באַהויכט
מיט גרינעם זומער און מיט טוי,
און נאָך,
און נאָך
מסתם מיט גאָט,
װייל אויסער גאָט קאָן גוט נישט זיין אזוי.

כ'געדענק איצט אַלץ:
אַ פערד, װאָס איז געפאַלן אויפן ברוק,
די נויט,
מיין ברודער, דעם אָפגעזאָגטן קנעכט,
זיין קאָפּ, װאָס גרויט.


## VEN S'BLIAKEVET MAYN OYG

Ven s'bliakevet mayn oyg,
iz gut, vos s'blaybt der himl bloy,
un s'iz der vald bahoykht
mit grinem zumer un mit toy,
un nokh,
un nokh
mestam mit got,
vayl oyser got kon gut nisht zayn azoy.

Kh'gedenk itst alts:
a ferd, vos iz gefaln oyfn bruk,
di noyt,
mayn bruder, dem opgezogtn knekht,
zayn kop, vos groyt.

# 2

# KADIE MOLODOWSKY

## WHEN MY EYE LOSES ITS HUE

When my eye loses its hue,
it is good that the sky stays blue,
and the forest is ruled
by green summer and by dew,
and too,
and too,
probably by God,
for without God such good cannot be.

I now remember all:
a horse that stumbled on the road,
the pauper-days,
my brother, the rejected slave,
his head that greys.

מײַן גאַס,
מײַן גאַס, וואָס איז דורכויס ווי איך אַליין,
אין שמאַטעס אָנגעטאָן,
אין   מאָרגנדיקן טאָג פֿאַרטרויט.
דעם אַלטן אויפֿן ראָג,
זײַן פּנים ווי אַן אָפּגעשטעלטער זייגער,
פּונקט אַזוי אַשטייגער,
ווי די זאָקן, וואָס ער פֿאַרקויפֿט,
וואָלטן געווען באַא־שלאַנגען,
און ביזן גאָרגל האָבן זיי אַרויפֿגעוויקלט זיך,
דערגאַנגען.

נאָר גרינער וואַלד איז גרין,
און יונגע זשאַבקעס זענען וואונדער,
און זענען גאָט,
פּונקט ווי ראַדיאָ
און ווי לבֿנה און טשערת.


*Mayn gas,*
*mayn gas, vos iz durkhoys vi ikh aleyn,*
*in shmates ongeton,*
*in morgndikn tog fartroyt.*
*Dem altn oyfn rog,*
*zayn ponem vi an opgeshtelter zeyger,*
*punkt azoy ashteyger,*
*vi di zokn, vos er farkoyft,*
*voltn geven boa-shlangen,*
*un bizn gorgl hobn zey aroyfgeviklt zikh,*
*dergangen.*

*Nor griner vald is grin,*
*un yunge zhabkes zenen vunder,*
*un zenen got,*
*punkt vi radio*
*un vi levone un tsherot.*

**2**

My street,
my street, completely like me,
in rags arrayed,
pawned to the coming day.
The old man on the corner,
his face like a run-down clock,
just exactly
as if the stockings that he sells
were boa snakes,
and winding themselves up to his throat,
constricted.

But the green forest is green,
and young frogs are miracles,
and are God,
just like radio
and moon and reeds.

# טעקסט

מיר אלע —
שטיינער, מענטשן, שערבלעך גלאז אין זון,
קאנסערוון־פושקעס, קעץ און ביימער —
זענען אילוסטראציעס צו א טעקסט.

ערגעץ־וואו דארף מען אונדז נישט האבן.
דארט לייענט מען דעם טעקסט אליין —
די בילדער פאלן אפ ווי טויטע גלידער.

ווען טויט־ווינט גיט א בלאז אין טיפן גראז
און רוימט־אראפ פון מערב אלע בילדער,
וואס וואלקנס האבן אויפגעשטעלט —
קומט נאכט און לייענט שטערן.

*TEKST*

*Mir ale —*
*shteyner, mentshn, sherblekh gloz in zun,*
*konservn-pushkes, kets un beymer —*
*zenen ilustratsies tsu a tekst.*

*Ergets-vu darf men undz nisht hobn,*
*dort leyent men dem tekst aleyn —*
*di bilder faln op vi toyte glider.*

*Ven toyt-vint git a bloz in tifn groz*
*un roymt arop fun mayrev ale bilder,*
*vos volkns hobn oyfgeshtelt —*
*kumt nakht un leyent shtern.*

# 3

# AARON ZEITLIN

## TEXT

All of us —
stones, people, glass slivers in the sun,
tin cans, cats, and trees —
are illustrations for a text.

Someplace, somewhere we are not needed;
there the text alone is read —
the pictures drop away like dead limbs.

When death-wind blows through deep grass
and sweeps from the west all pictures
that clouds have raised —
the night comes and reads stars.

## ווי דורך גרין-באַגראָזטע פעלדער . . .

ווי דורך גרין באַגראָזטע פעלדער
עם וואַנדערט פייפנדיק דער הירט,
ווי אין די אלטע, טיפע וועלדער
דער לעצטער זונשיין זיך פאַרלירט;

די מילדע, גאָלדענע פאַרנאַכטן;
דער ים, ווען ס׳קומט די זון אַרויס;
דאָס אינגליש אומשולדיקע שמאַכטן,
דאָס וואַרטן פאַר דער ליבסטערס הויז;

ווי ס׳קעמפט דאָס פאָלק און פאָנען וויען
אויף באַריקאַדן בלוטיק רויט —
אין קינעמאטאָגראַף צו זען
בין איך דאָס אַלעם שטענדיק גרייט.

## VI DURKH GRIN-BAGROZTE FELDER . . .

Vi durkh grin bagrozte felder
es vandert fayfndik der hirt,
vi in di alte, tife velder
der letster zunshayn zikh farlirt;

di milde, goldene farnakhtn;
der yam, ven s'kumt di zun aroys;
dos yinglish umshuldike shmakhtn,
dos vartn far der libsters hoyz;

vi s'kemft dos folk un fonen veyen
oyf barikadn blutik royt —
in kinematograf tsu zen
bin ikh dos alles shtendik greyt.

# 4

## ZISHA LANDAU

## HOW THROUGH GREEN-GRASSED FIELDS

How through green-grassed fields
the whistling shepherd strays;
how in the old deep-wooded forest
are lost the last sun's rays;

the mild, golden twilights,
the sea, when the sun comes out;
the boyish innocent longings,
the waiting at the loved one's house;

how people fight, and on barricades
flags wave blood red over the scene —
these things I am always ready
to watch — on a cinema screen.

# איבער אלע דעכער

איבער אלע דעכער
הענגט אַ שטילע נאַכט
אָנגעלענט ביים פענסטער
שטייט מיין קינד פֿאַרטראַכט.

שטעלט זיך אויף די פינגער
קוקט און קוקט אַרוים,
זיין געזיכט ווערט בלאַסער,
און די אויגן גרוים.

זיינע בלאָנדע לאָקן,
קרייזלען זיך אין ווינט. —
ווייס איין גוטער גאָט נאָר,
וואָס עס טראַכט מיין קינד.

## IBER ALE DEKHER

*Iber ale dekher,*
*hengt a shtile nakht*
*ongelent baym fenster*
*shteyt mayn kind fartrakht.*

*Shtelt zikh oyf di finger*
*kukt un kukt aroys,*
*zayn gezikht vert blaser,*
*un di oygn groys.*

*Zayne blonde lokn,*
*krayzlen zikh in vint. —*
*Veys eyn guter got nor,*
*vos es trakht mayn kind.*

# 5

## REUBEN ICELAND

### OVER ALL THE ROOF TOPS

Over all the roof tops
a quiet night is posed.
Leaning at the window
my child stands engrossed,

gets up on his tiptoes,
peers and peers outside;
his face grows paler
and his eyes grow wide.

His blond ringlets
curl in the breeze.
The good God alone knows
what my child sees.

# שטילע טריט אין װײכן מאָך

שטילע טריט אין װײכן מאָך,
שבת-רו אַ גאַנצע װאָך.


אַלע אָװנט צינדסטו ליכט —
ראָזער שײן אױף דײן געזיכט.


דורך דעם גרינעם סאָסנע-סכך
בלױט אדורך גאָטס בלױער דאַך.


דאָרט צינדט אױך װער שבת-ליכט, —
שאָטנס בלױ אױף דײן געזיכט.


זיצן מיר און האַלטן װאַכט,
װאַרטן אױף אַ װאונדער-נאַכט.


## SHTILE TRIT IN VEYKHN MOKH

*Shtile trit in veykhn mokh,*
*shabes-ru a gantse vokh.*

*Ale ovnt tsindstu likht —*
*rozer shayn oyf dayn gezikht.*

*Durkh dem grinem sosne-skhakh*
*bloyt adurkh gots bloyer dakh.*

*Dort tsindt oykh ver shabes-likht, —*
*shotns bloy oyf dayn gezikht.*

*Zitsn mir un haltn vakht,*
*vartn oyf a vunder-nakht.*

# 6

# DAVID EINHORN

## IN SOFT MOSS, MUTED STEPS

In soft moss, muted steps,
a whole week of Sabbath rest.

You light candles every night —
your face in rosy light.

Between the green pine tree boughs
the blue of God's blue roof top shows.

There too someone lights Sabbath tapers —
on your face blue shadows vapor.

So we sit, keeping watch,
waiting for a wonder night.

גייט אַ רוישן דורכן וואַלד,
שפּאַלט דער הימל זיך און שטראַלט.

שטילע טריט אין ווייכן מאָך,
שבת-רו אַ גאַנצע וואָך.

יעדן אָוונט צינדסטו ליכט, —
ראָזער שיין אויף דיין געזיכט.

Geyt a royshn durkhn vald,
shpalt der himl zikh un shtralt.

Shtile trit in veykhn mokh,
shabes-ru a gantse vokh.

Yedn ovnt tsindstu likht, —
rozer shayn oyf dayn gezikht.

**6**

Through the forest a rustle goes,
the sky splits apart and glows.

In soft moss, muted steps,
a whole week of Sabbath rest.

You light candles every night —
your face in rosy light.

# דער זינגער

שווינדלט אַ שטוב און אַ וועג און אַ באַן,
און אַלע דערצײלן, אַז דו ביסט פֿאַראַן, ביסט פֿאַראַן, ביסט פֿאַראַן.

נאָר ס'קומט אַ זינגער אין הויף, וואו איך וואוין, (זינגט אַן אַלטן סאָנעט)
כאַפּ איך זיך אויף: איך זיץ דאָך בײַ זיך אויפֿן בעט.

און איך זע: עס איז זון, און דער הימל איז בלאָ,
נאָר קיין וועג איז נישטאָ, איז נישטאָ, איז נישטאָ.

זינגט דער זינגער אַ ליד: ווי אַ ייִנגל האָט ליב, ווי אַ מיידל האָט ליב,
נויג איך אים מיטן קאָפּ: עס איז אמת דײַן ליד, ווי גאָלד איז דײַן ליד.

און איך זאָג: נעם מיך מיט אין דײַן גאַנג,
וועל איך קומען אַהין, ווי עס וויל מײַן פֿאַרלאַנג.

## DER ZINGER

*Shvindlt a shtub un a veg un a ban,*
*un ale dertseyln, az du bist faran, bist faran, bist faran.*

*Nor s'kumt a zinger in hoyf, vu ikh voyn, (zingt an altn*
    *sonet)*
*khap ikh zikh oyf: ikh zits dokh bay zikh oyfn bet.*

*Un ikh ze: es iz zun, un der himl iz blo,*
*nor kayn veg iz nishto, iz nishto, iz nishto.*

*Zingt der zinger a lid: vi a yingl hot lib, vi a meydl hot lib,*
*noyg ikh im mitn kop: es iz emes dayn lid, vi gold is dayn lid.*

*Un ikh zog: nem mikh mit in dayn gang,*
*vel ikh kumen ahin, vi es vil mayn farlang.*

# KADIE MOLODOWSKY

## THE SINGER

A house and a road and a train reel in air,
and all of them say, you are there, you are there, you are there.

A singer comes into the yard where I live (sings an old
    sonnet),
I wake from my sleep: this is my own bed, I am still in it.

And I see: there is sun, and the heavens are clear,
but the road is not here, is not here, is not here.

The singer sings: of a boy in love, of a girl in love.
My head nods to him: true is your song, like gold is your song.

Will you take me along on your road, I enquire,
so I may come there, where my wishes aspire?

זאָגט דער זינגער צו מיר: ביסט אַ קינד, ביסט אַ נאַר,
זעסט דעם פויגל, וואָס פליט?
איך באַדאַרף נאָר זיין פלי, און דיין צער פאַר מיין ליד.

און איך זע: עס איז זון, און דער הימל איז בלאָ,
נאָר קיין וועג איז נישטאָ, איז נישטאָ, איז נישטאָ.

*Zogt der zinger tsu mir: bist a kind, bist a nar, zest dem*
   *foygl, vos flit?*
*Ikh badarf nor zayn fli, un dayn tsar far mayn lid.*

*Un ikh ze: es iz zun, un der himl iz blo,*
*nor kayn veg iz nishto, iz nishto, iz nishto.*

# 7

Says the singer to me: You're a child, you're a fool; see the
  bird that flies?
I need only his flight, and your woe, my song to devise.

And I see: there is sun, and the heavens are clear,
but the road is not here, is not here, is not here.

אין פעלד האט גענומען שוין ציען מיט נעפלען פון אסיען . . .
ארוים איז דער זיידע פארטאג צום געמויזעכץ דאָס היי אראָפּקאָסיען,
איז מען ביים שאַריען אויף טאָג שוין געווען ביגלופֿין, אזוי ווי
די אמתע קלעזמער,
מען האט זיך צעשטעלט זאַלבעצענט, דער זיידע בראָש, און אַוועק
אין אַ מזמור:
אַ שפּרייז, און אַ קער מיט די פּלייצעס, אַ סוווישטש, פּונקט עס
טאַנצן אין זומפּ ארום בליצן,
פֿאר דאָס שטיקעלע ברויט — האָט דער זיידע געזאָגט — מוז מען,
קינדערלעך, שוויצן . . .
און ס׳האָבן זיך בלאַנקער די קאָסעס צעפֿייפֿט, די קאַפּאָטעס אַראָפּ,
מיט באַוואַקסענע גלידער,
אזוי ווי די האַריקע יאָדלעס — אַ טאַטע אַן אַלטער מיט זיבעצן
לייבלעכע ברידער . . .


# MEN KOSYET HEY . . .

*In feld hot genumen shoyn tsien mit neplen fun osyen . . .*
*aroys iz der zeyde fartog tsum gemoyzekhts dos hey*
*aropkosyen.*
*Iz men baym sharyen oyf tog shoyn geven biglufin, azoy vi*
*di emese klezmer,*
*men hot zikh tseshtelt zalbetsent, der zeyde berosh, un avek*
*in a mizmer.*
*A shprayz, un a ker mit di pleytses, a svishtsh, punkt es*
*tantsn in zump arum blitsn,*
*far dos shtikele broyt — hot der zeyde gezogt — muz men,*
*kinderlekh, shvitsn . . .*
*Un s'hobn zikh blanker di koses tsefayft, di kapotes arop,*
*mit bavaksene glider,*
*azoy vi di horike yodles — a tate an alter mit zibetsn*
*layblekhe brider . . .*

# 8

# MOYSHE KULBAK

## HAY MOWING

Over the fields the autumn mist had begun to stray.
Grandfather left at dawn for the marsh to mow the hay.
At the raking, when day came, like jolly musicians dazed
they stood in tens, grandfather first, and sang a psalm of
    praise.
A step, a twist of the shoulders, a whistle, as if swamp-
    lightning leapt.
For a piece of bread, children (my grandfather spoke), one
    has to sweat.
And the scythes whistled more brightly; coats off, with
    hairy limbs
like the hairy firs — an old father with seventeen blood-
    brothers . . .

עס צופן די קאסעס, ס'צעשפריצט זיך דער טוי, און עס פאלן
די גרעזער אויף גרעזער אנידער,
א פייגעלע זינגט אויף א נוס־בוים דערביי, אז דער זיידע קאן פשוט
קיין ארט ניט געפינען:
"װאָס זאָגסטו דערצו? נא דיר גאר א קאנאריק, א חזן, אינמיטן
דערינען"...
דאָ נעמט מען זיך טאָטשען די קאסעס, פאררוייכערט מען,
כאפט מען א זופעלע קװאס פונעם קריגל,
דערנאָך שטייט מען אויף מיט א קרעכץ... פּאָמאָהײ באָך!
א קלונג, און עס טוט זיך די קאסע א שפּיגל,
באַװייזט זיך, פאַרשװינדט צװישן גראָז, טוט א בלאַנק —
אַכצן קאסעס כסדר!...

*Es tsupn di koses, s'tseshpritst zikh der toy, un es faln di*
*grezer oyf grezer anider,*
*a feygele zingt oyf a nus-boym derbay, az der zeyde kon*
*poshet kayn ort nit gefinen:*
*"Vos zogstu dertsu? Na dir gor a kanarik, a khazn inmitn*
*derinen."*
*Do nemt men zikh totshen di koses, faroykhert men, khapt*
*men a zupele kvas funem krigl,*
*dernokh shteyt men oyf mit a krekhts ... Pomohey bokh! A*
*klung, un es tut zikh di kose a shpigl,*
*bavayzt zikh, farshvinat tsvishn groz, tut a blank — akhtsn*
*koses keseyder! ...*

**8**

The scythes twitch, dew spurts out, and the grasses fall, one
    on the other.
A bird sings in a nut tree nearby; grandfather cannot be
    serene:
"What do you say to that? A canary, a cantor, right on the
    scene!"
Now they sharpen their scythes, smoke, grab a sip from the
    pitcher,
then arise with a groan . . . "Pomohey bokh!" A clang, and
    the scythe is all glitter.
Appears, disappears in the grass, blazes out — eighteen
    scythes in order.

און ס'בויגן זיך זיכער די הענט, אָ, עס קנאָקן די שענקלען,

און פעסט זיצט אַ יעטוועדער גדר — — —

אַזוי ביז דער עולם דערזעט, ווי דער רויטער פֿאַרנאַכט לייכט

זיך אָפֿ אין די קאָסעס,

טוט חברה אַ שמייכל. מען זעט שוין דעם הערינג דעם ברייטן,

דער באָבעשיס קעז־סאַלטענאָסעס,

דערלאַנגט מען אַ נעם די קאַפּאָטעס, מע גייט און מע הערט

צו די וואַכטלען, וואָס שרייען,

מע גייט מיט די קאָסעס, פֿאַרלייגט אויף די פּלייצעס, מע קוקט

און מע שוווייגט, ווי די שלייען . . .

פּאָמאָהיי באָך!: העלף, גאָט!

Un s'boygn zikh zikher di hent, o, es knakn di shenklen, un
  fest zitst a yetveder geder.
Azoy biz der oylem derzet, vi der royter farnakht laykht
  zikh op in di koses,
tut khevre a shmeykhl. Men zet shoyn dem hering dem
  breytn, der bobeshis kez-saltenoses.
Derlangt men a nem di kapotes, me geyt un me hert tsu di
  vakhtln, vos shrayen,
me geyt mit di koses, farleygt oyf di pleytses, me kukt un
  me shvaygt, vi di shlayen.

Pomohey bokh: helf, got!

**8**

And the hands bend with sureness, the legs crack, and
    sturdily rises each border —
until all of them see the red twilight dim on their scythes
    and decrease,
and all of them smile. They can see the broad herring and
    grandma's pancakes of cheese.
They throw on their coats, they walk along listening to the
    quails shout.
With their scythes on their shoulders they gaze and are
    mute as the trout.

Pomohey bokh: Polish "Help, God!"

# מען טרייבט פליטן . . .

עס האָבן די נעפלען פֿאַרוישט און פֿאַרשמירט אַלע דערפֿער און וועגן,
אין פֿעלד טאַפּט מען אָן מיטן וואַרעמן פּנים די קאַלטקייט פֿון
העגנגעדן רעגן . . .

עס וויזן זיך פֿלעקן פֿון ביימער, פֿון ערגעץ אַ הויף, אַן אַסוויר
פֿון אַ ברונען,

נאָר ס׳שוויםט עפּעס אָן, עס ווערט ווייס פֿאַר די אויגן . . . און אַלץ
ווערט אין נעפּל צערונען.

אַ טרוקענער צוויג פֿאַלט אַראָפּ. עס איז שטיל. אַ פֿויגל
הייבט אָנעט צו קלאָגן:

״ס׳קומט אויסעט אין לעבן אַזויפֿיל אַריבערצוטראָגן, אַזויפֿיל
אַריבערצוטראָגן״ . . .

די צענדליקער קוועלכעלעך פּליעסקענען צווישן די בייטן און
מורמלען און ריידן,

און צווישן די נעפּלען ווייט-ווייט אויפֿן ניעמאַן דערהערט זיך
די שטים פֿונעם זיידן:

## MEN TRAYBT PLITN . . .

*Es hobn di neplen farvisht un farshmirt ale derfer un vegn,*
*in feld tapt men on mitn varemn ponem di kaltkayt fun*
 *hengendn regn . . .*
*Es vayzn zikh flekn fun beymer, fun ergets a hoyf, an asvir*
 *fun a brunen,*
*nor s'shvimpt epes on, es vert vays far di oygn . . . un alts vert*
 *in nepl tserunen.*
*A trukener tsvayg falt arop. Es iz shtil. A foygl heybt onet tsu*
 *klogn:*
*"S'kumt oyset in lebn azoyfil aribertsutrogn, azoyfil ariber-*
 *tsutrogn" . . .*
*Di tsendliker kvelkhelekh pliyeskenen tsvishn di baytn un*
 *murmlen un reydn,*
*un tsvishn di neplen vayt-vayt oyfn Nyeman derhert zikh di*
 *shtim funem zeydn:*

# 9

# MOYSHE KULBAK

## DRIVING THE RAFTS

The mists have erased and smudged every road, every town.
In the field your warm face meets the cold of rain coming
   down.
Blotches of tree, of some yard, the pulley on a well, touch
   your gaze,
but something swims up, your eye faces white — in the mist
   all is haze.
A withered branch falls. It is quiet. A bird sings in despair:
"In this life there is so much to endure, so much to bear" . . .
Tens of rivulets splashing in their beds chattered and mur-
   mured;
through the far-far mists on the Neman grandfather's voice is
   heard:

שמוליע, העי, שמוליע,

פֿאַרפּאַטשט דעם הינטן אויף סקאַרוליע! ...

דער זיידע קריכט אום מיט אַ באָרד מיט אַ נאָסער און טאַפּט
די שוואַרצועס,

די פֿעטערס אין נעפּל מיט לאַנגע בוסאַקעס מען שפּרייזט אויף
די פּליטן,

אָט ווערן זיי נעלם. מען הערט נאָר אַרוים פֿון דער זייט
דעם געשריִענעם שמועס,

עס טוען אַ פּליעסק אָפּאַטשינעס, אַ גראָב, און דער שטראָם
ווערט צעשניטן ...

דער נעפּל פֿילט אויסעט די ליימיקע ברענן, ניטאָ — ניט קיין ערד,
ניט קיין וואַסער.

און ווייך איז די געגנט אַזוי, און ממשות — אַ וואַרעמער אָטעם
אַ בלאָסער ...


Shmulye, hey, Shmulye,
farpatsh dem hintn oyf skarulye! ...
Der zeyde krikht um mit a bord mit a naser un tapt di
      shvartsues,
di feters in nepl mit lange busakes men shprayzt oyf di plitn,
ot vern zey nelem. Men hert nor aroys fun zayt dem geshri-
      yenem shmues,
es tuen a pliyesk opatshines, a grob, un der shtrom vert
      tseshnitn ...
Der nepl filt oyset di leymike bregn, nito — nit kayn erd, nit
      kayn vaser.
Un veykh iz der gegnt azoy, un mamoshes — a varemer otem
      a blaser ...

**9**

"Shmulye, hey Shmulye.
Slap your rear toward shore."
Grandfather, wet-bearded, crawls about and fingers the barges.
In the mist, the uncles with long hooks step over the rafts.
Now they vanish. Off on one side their shouted talk emerges.
The sinkers splash, a hole, the river is slashed.
The mist fills up the clay banks, there is no water, there is no
    land,
and the region is so soft, its texture — a breath warm and
    bland . . .

נאָר ס'וויקלט זיך עפּעס . . . אָט גייען די כלערליי טאָלן און
וועלדער אַריבער,
דאָרט שטייען פאַרוויקלט די הייזער, נאַקעטע ווי מעבל אין
גבירישע שטיבער . . .
און אָט פּלאַצט דאָ אויפעט אַ קלאָרקייט אַ גרינע . . . ס'ווערט
קלערער ביי זיך אין נשמה . . .
די זון טוט אַ לייכט. עס באַוויזט זיך דאָס וואַסער און וועּרבעֲס,
פאַרוויינטע און לאָמע,
דער וואַלד האָט זיך בלויז אויסגעוואַשן, איז נאַס, און דער קאָפּ
זיינער פלאַקערט,
און ס'גייט זיך אַ העלקייט וויַיט־וויַיט אויף אַ לאָנקע . . . אַ פּויערל
שטייט דאָרט און אַקערט . .

Nor s'viklt zikh epes ... ot geyen di kolerley toln un velder
    aribet,
dort shteyen farviklt di hayzer, nakete vi mebl in gvirishe
    shtiber ...
Un ot platst do oyfet a klorkayt a grine ... s'vert klerer bay
    zikh in neshome ...
Di zun tut a laykht. Es bavayzt zikh dos vaser un verbes, far-
    veynte un lome,
der vald hot zikh bloyz oysgevashn, iz nas, un der kop zayner
    flakert,
un s'geyt zikh a helkayt vayt-vayt oyf a lonke ... a poyerl
    shteyt dort un akert ...

.

**9**

but something is unfolding . . . the manifold valleys and forests
    loom.
There houses stand shrouded in bareness, furniture in a rich
    man's room.
Here green lucidity bursts open . . . even one's soul grows
    clear.
The sun shines forth. Water and lame weeping willows
    appear.
The forest has taken a bath, is wet, and his head is a flare,
and brightness walks far off in a meadow . . . a peasant plows
    there.

א רחבות, א פרישקייט פון גראָזיקע לאָנקעם, וואָס שמעקן
און פינקלען און וויינען,
און ס'שוויִמען נאָך אומעט די שטיקער פון נעפלען — חלומות
פון פעלדער און פּליינען . . .
און ס'שוויִמען די פּליטן געלאָסן, געלאָסן, פֿאַרקירעוועןֹ רונד
מיט די ברעגן,
די שטרוֹיענע ביַידלעך שטראַלן און פאָרען אַרויסעט דעם טוי
און דעם רעגן.
דערביַי ליגט דער זיַידע . . . ער רויכערט די לולקע און זשמורעט
פון תּענוג די אויגן:
די וואַרעמע ערד האָט זיך גלאַנציק און פעט אזוי שטאַרק אויסגעצויגן,
צעקעסטלט אין פעלדער, געמויזעכצן, געלבע און העלע און גרינע —
עס גיסט זיך דער דורכזיכטיק-ציטריקער פלאַקס אויף בורשטיניקע
שטענגלעך דינע,
די גרינקייט אויף פעלדער-קאַרטאָפל ליגט אָפּגעקילט, מאַט,
אויסגעזאָטן . . .
און ס'שמייכלט די קורצע די ראָזעווע רעטשקע מיט שפּרענקעלעך
וויַיסע באַשאָטן —

A rakhves, a frishkayt fun grozike lonkes, vos shmekn un
finklen un veynen,
un s'shvimen nokh umet di shtiker fun neplen — khaloymes
fun felder un pleynen . . .
Un s'shvimen di plitn gelasn, gelasn, farkireven rund mit di
bregn,
di shtroyene baydlekh shtraln un porn aroyset dem toy un
dem regn.
Derbay ligt der zeyde . . . Er roykhert di lulke un zhmuret fun
tanig di oygn:
di vareme erd hot zikh glantsik un fet azoy shtark oysgetsoygn,
tsekestlt in felder, gemoyzekhtsn, gelbe un hele un grine —
es gist zikh der durkhzikhtik-tsitriker flaks oyf burshtinike
shtenglekh dine,
di grinkayt oyf felder-kartofl ligt opgekilt, mat, oysgezotn . . .
un s'shmeykhlt di kurtse di rozeve retshke mit shprenkelekh
vayse bashotn —

**9**

A lushness, a freshness of grass meadows that smell, shimmer, complain,
and scraps of mist still swim about — the dreams of field and plain . . .
Slowly, slowly the rafts float, swing round with the shores of the stream.
The straw huts radiate their moisture and rain into steam.
There rests Grandfather, smoking his pipe and squinting his eyes in delight.
The warm earth has lustily stretched itself out, all plump and bright,
checkered by fields, by marshes yellow and lucent and green.
The transparent trembling flax tumbles over on its stalks, amber and thin.
The green on field-potatoes lies opaque, limp, exhausted,
and the short pink buckwheat smiles with white speckles frosted.

עס רינען די זאַפֿטן פֿון דרערד, אַז אַ שיכּרות נעמט דורך אַלע גלידער,

עס שפּאַרט זיך אַ לעבן אַ שטומער דורך גרעזער, דורך װאָרצלען
און צװייגן,

אַז ס׳האַלט מער ניט אױסעט דער זיידע, ער טוט זיך אַ נעם,

אָ, ער קאָן מער ניט שװייגן,

דערלאַנגט ער אַ רעװע: טראַסטסיאַ אין דיין טאַטן! און
נאָכאַמאָל װידער:

טראַסטסיאַ אין דיין מאַמען! אַז ס׳כאַפּן זיך אױפֿעט די זין אױף די פּליטן,

מען זעט, אַז עס פֿלייצן אַראָפּ פֿון די פֿעלדער די פֿאַרבן די הייסע,
װי שטראָמען.

עס שפּרודלט פֿון פֿרילינג אַריין אױף דער װעלט און אַליין איז מען
אױך דאָ אינמיטן ...

רבונו של עולם! עס טוט זיך דאָ װאָס אױף די פֿעלדער,
װאָס האָט ניט קיין נאָמען! ...

— — — — — — — — — —

— — — — — — — — —

*Es rinen di zaftn fun drerd, az a shikres nemt durkh ale glider.*
*Es shpart zikh a lebn a shtumer durkh grezer, durkh vortslen*
*un tsvaygn,*
*az s'halt mer nit oyset der zeyde, er tut zikh a nem, o, er kon*
*mer nit shvaygn,*
*derlangt er a reve: Trastsya in dayn tatn! Un nokhamol vider:*
*Trastsya in dayn mamen! Az s'khapn zikh oyfet di zin oyf di*
*plitn,*
*men zet az es fleytsn arop fun di felder di farbn di heyse, vi*
*shtromen.*
*Es shprudlt fun friling arayn oyf der velt un aleyn iz men oykh*
*do inmitn ...*
*Reboynoy shel oylom! Es tut zikh do vos oyf di felder, vos hot*
*nit kayn nomen! ..*

— — — — — — — — — —

— — — — — — — — —

**9**

The earth-saps are rising, in the body drunkenness reigns.
A voiceless life thrusts through grass, through root and
    through tendril.
Grandfather can no longer bear it, o, he cannot keep still.
He bellows: "May your father have the tremors!" And once
    more again:
"May your mother have the tremors!" The sons on their
    barges jump up,
they see, from the fields are flowing in streams hot colors of
    flame.
The world is sprouting with Spring, and they too are right
    at its hub.
Lord of the Universe — on these fields something is happen-
    ing that has no name!

אַזוי האָט דער זיידעניו, עליו-השלום, די פּליטן געטריבן קיין פּרייסן,

איז ער פֿאַרנאַכטלעך אַריין מיט דער בלויער ווילִיע אין ניעמאַן
אין ווייסן,

האָט מען די שריגעס פֿאַרגראָבן אין זאַמד און די שווערע
שוואַרצועס פֿאַרבונדן,

און פֿייערן האָבן די פֿעטערס אויף יעטוועדער פּליט אָנגעצונדן.

שווייגעוודיק-מיד, זאַלבעצוויית בײַ אַ פֿייער, אַזוי איז מען
גרויע געזעסן.

געבראָכן דעם ראָזעווען ברויט און דעם באָרשט פונעם טעפּל געגעסן.


ס׳איז שטיל אויפֿן געגנט געוועזן. עס האָבן נאָר בלויע
וועלן געזונגען,

עס האָט נאָר דער פֿייער זיך הילכיק צעבלעטלט, צעלייגט,
ווי אַ רויטינקער בלימל,

און ס׳איז נאָר אַ פֿיש ווען ניט ווען פונעם וואַסער דעם קילן
געשפּרונגען.

בלוי איז געוועזן, און אַ רויטע לבֿנה, אַ שווערע, איז אַרויס אויפֿן הימל.



*Azoy hot der zeydenyu, olov hasholem, di plitn getribn kayn
Praysn,*

*iz er farnakhtlekh arayn mit der bloyer Vilye in Nyeman in
vaysn,*

*hot men di shriges fargrobn in zamd un di shvere shvartsues
farbundn,*

*un fayern hobn di feters oyf yetveder plit ongetsundn.*

*Shvaygevdik-mid, zalbetsveyt bay a fayer, azoy iz men groye
gezesn.*

*Gebrokhn dem rozeven broyt un dem borsht funem tepl
gegesn.*

*S'iz shtil oyfn gegnt gevezn. Es hobn nor bloye veln gezungen,*

*es hot nor der fayer zikh hilkhik tsebletlt, tseleygt, vi a
roytinker bliml,*

*un s'iz nor a fish ven nit ven funem vaser dem kiln ge-
shprungen.*

*Bloy iz geven, un a royte levone, a shvere, iz aroys oyfn himl.*

**9**

So Grandfather, may he rest in peace, the rafts into Prussia
    floated,
and at twilight from the blue Vilija into the white Neman
    boated.
The anchors were buried in sand, the heavy barges
    tied,
and on each of the barges my uncles lit fires.
Mute with fatigue, two to a fire, so they sat
    greyed.
Broke the rose-colored bread and ate the borsht from
    a pot.

It was quiet in the region. Only the blue waves sang;
only the echoing fire leafed out, a red flower, and
    spread,
and once in a while in the water a fish
    sprang.
It was blue, and a red moon, ponderous, rose overhead.

ONIONS AND CUCUMBERS AND PLUMS

M. L. Halpern was one of the finest and most influential of the American Yiddish poets. His sense of fantasy and romanticism is balanced, as in "Never Again Will I Say," against an alertness to the coarseness and poverty of Jewish urban life. His self-chastisement —good manners and gentility are luxuries, he reminds himself —is almost painfully objectified in the poem. Jacob Glatstein describes in "Biography" what will emerge as accomplishments in his other poems translated here. He writes freely and broadly about his world, and brings sophistication made clumsy (and moving) by anger to bear on that world. Itzik Manger has used with immense skill the folk song line in his poetry, and "Love" indicates some of the staple members of the cast of most of his poems: love, death, a mother, small animals, God. Kulbak's poems about his grandmother belong to the same series as the one about his grandfather and here shift their form and tone to bring us the quieter image of the almost-classic Jewish mother (recorded so well by Avrom Reisen): hard-working, patient, pious, loving. Molodowsky's "The Mother" is waiting for a daughter who has been imprisoned for revolutionary activities, a familiar enough situation for the European family. Sutskever's "Father Dies" mentions the "fiddle white as quartz." The violin appears in many Yiddish poems, the instrument of piercing tears, of sustained pain, and of jigging gaiety.

קיינמאָל שוין וועל איך נישט זאָגן

פאַראַנען לײט וואָס קענען אפשר זאָגן
אז ס'איז ניט שײן, צו שטופּן זיך אַרום אַ וואָגן
מיט ציבעלעס, און אוגערקעס, און פלוימען.
נאָר אז ס'איז שײן אין מיטן גאַס זיך נאָכשלעפּן אַ טױטנוואָגן —
אָנגעטאָן אין שוואַרצן, און צו דעם נאָך קלאָגן,
איז דאָך אַ זינד צו זאָגן
אז ס'איז ניט שײן, צו שטופּן זיך אַרום אַ וואָגן
מיט ציבעלעס, און אוגערקעס, און פלוימען.

# KEYNMOL SHOYN VEL IKH NISHT ZOGN

*Faranen layt vos kenen efsher zogn*
*az s'iz nit sheyn, tsu shtupn zikh arum a vogn*
*mit tsibeles, un ugerkes, un floymn.*
*Nor az s'iz sheyn in mitn gas zikh nokhshlepn a toytnvogn —*
*onegton in shvartsn, un tsu dem nokh klogn,*
*iz dokh a zind tsu zogn*
*az s'iz nit sheyn, tsu shtupn zikh arum a vogn*
*mit tsibeles, un ugerkes, un floymn.*

# 10

# MOYSHE LEYB HALPERN

## NEVER AGAIN WILL I SAY

There are people who perhaps would say
it is not polite to crowd around a dray
of onions and cucumbers and plums.
But if it is polite to trail after a hearse, in the middle of
    the street,
dressed all in black, and moreover weep,
then it is a sin to say
it is not polite to crowd around a dray
of onions and cucumbers and plums.

מע דאַרף אפשר נישט רײַסן זיך אזוי, און שלאָגן.
מע קען דאָך רואיק שטופּן זיך ארום אַ װאָגן
מיט ציבעלעס, און אוגערקעס, און פֿלוימען.
נאָר אז סע קען די בײַטש אפֿילו קײנעם נישט פֿאַריאָגן,
װײַל דער טיראַן פֿון דעם באַשעפֿעניש אױף דר'ערד, דער מאָגן
װיל אזוי — באַדאַרף מען שױן אַ רשע זײַן, צו זאָגן
אז ס'איז ניט שײן צו שטופּן זיך ארום אַ װאָגן
מיט ציבעלעס, און אוגערקעס, און פֿלוימען.

דאַריבער טאַקע װעל איך קײנמאָל שױן נישט זאָגן
אז ס'איז ניט שײן צו שטופּן זיך ארום אַ װאָגן
מיט ציבעלעס, און אוגערקעס, און פֿלוימען.
װי שטאַרק עס זאָל אַ שטופּעניש אזאַ, מיך מאַטערן און פּלאָגן,
װעל איך מײַן קאָפּ אַרונטערבױגן, און אַריבערטראָגן.
װײַנען װעל איך אפשר — אָבער קײנמאָל שױן װעל איך ניט זאָגן
אז ס'איז ניט שײן צו שטופּן זיך ארום אַ װאָגן
מיט ציבעלעס, און אוגערקעס, און פֿלוימען.

*Me darf efsher nisht raysn zikh azoy, un shlogn,*
*me ken dokh ruik shtupn zikh arum a vogn*
*mit tsibeles, un ugerkes, un floymn.*
*Nor az se ken di baytsh afile keynem nisht faryogn,*
*vayl der tiran fun dem bashefenish oyf dr'erd, der mogn*
*vil azoy — badarf men shoyn a roshe zayn, tsu zogn*
*az s'iz nit sheyn tsu shtupn zikh arum a vogn*
*mit tsibeles, un ugerkes, un floymn.*

*Dariber take vel ikh keynmol shoyn nisht zogn*
*az s'iz nit sheyn tsu shtupn zikh arum a vogn*
*mit tsibeles, un ugerkes, un floymn.*
*Vi shtark es zol a shtupenish aza, mikh matern un plogn,*
*vel ikh mayn kop arunterboygn, un aribertrogn.*
*Veynen vel ikh efsher — ober keynmol shoyn vel ikh nit zogn*
*az s'iz nit sheyn tsu shtupn zikh arum a vogn*
*mit tsibeles, un ugerkes, un floymn.*

**10**

Maybe we shouldn't scramble so and fight;
we could at least shove quietly around the dray
of onions and cucumbers and plums.
But, since even a whip could chase not one of us away
because the tyrant of this earth's creatures, the stomach,
wants it so — you'd have to be a villain to say
it is not polite to crowd around a dray
of onions and cucumbers and plums.

For that very reason I'll never again say
it is not polite to crowd around a dray
of onions and cucumbers and plums.
However strongly such jostling may torment and trouble
    me
I will bow my head and bear it patiently.
I will weep perhaps — but I'll never again say
it is not polite to crowd around a dray
of onions and cucumbers and plums.

# דער טאטע שטארבט . . .

ס'פֿאלן אלע פֿארבן אָפּ. אײעדער
זון האָט הינטער זיך אַ װיסטן תּהום.
ס'לעשן זיך די שטראלנדיקסטע פֿעדעם
אין אַ קאלטן שטורעמדיקן שטראָם.
און מײַן טאטע זעט עס . . . זײַנע ברעמען
מעסערן זיך קעגן נאַכט און װינט.
זײַנע טיפֿע אויערן פֿאַרנעמען
דעם גערויש פֿון לעבן װאָס צעבינדט
אלע הייס פֿאַרפֿלאָכטענע געקנופּן.
און אין דאָרשט פֿון קיינמאָל-נישט-געשטילט, —
טרינקט ער שטומערהייט די לעצטע זופּן
פֿון דער צײַט. לבֿנהדיק און מילד.

# DER TATE SHTARBT ...

*S'faln ale farbn op. Ayeder*
*zun hot hinter zikh a vistn tehom.*
*S'leshn zikh di shtralndikste fedem*
*in a kaltn shturemdikn shtrom.*
*Un mayn tate zet es ... zayne bremen*
*mesern zikh kegn nakht un vint.*
*Zayne tife oyern farnemen*
*dem geroysh fun lebn vos tsebindt*
*ale heys farflokhtene geknupn.*
*Un in dorsht fun keynmol-nisht-geshtilt, —*
*trinkt er shtumerheyt di letste zupn*
*fun der tsayt. Levonedik un mild.*

# 11

# ABRAHAM SUTSKEVER

## FATHER DIES

All colors fade away. Beyond
every sun lies a barren pit.
The most lustrous threads drown
in a cold streaming flood.
And my father sees it; his brows
knife against the night and wind.
His deep ears absorb
the rush of life, unbinding
all hot entangled knots.
And with that never-ever-silenced thirst
he drinks mutely the last mouthfuls
of time. Moonlike and mild.

וייסקייט רונדאַרום. עס בלענדט דער געגנט,
ס'טראָגט זיך וואו דער כּוטער ווי אַ שוואַן.
טאַטע האָט מיט אַלץ זיך שוין געזעגנט.
איצט ליגט ער צוריק אויפן טאַפּטשאַן
און ער רעדט צו מיר מיטן ליבן שמייכל
ווערטער אומפֿאַרשטענדלעכע. איך ליג
שווייגיג אויפן דיל, און מאָדנע צייכנס
גיבן אין מיין טיפעניש אַ בליק:
צאַנקענדיקע פֿאַרבן — טאַטע — ייִנגל,
און אין פֿייערן דאָס יונגע האַרץ.
פֿון דעם שטילן אָוונטיקן ווינקל
וויינט אַראָפּ די פֿידל ווייס ווי קוואַרץ.

*Vayskayt rundarum. Es blendt der gegnt.*
*S'trogt zikh vu der khuter vi a shvan.*
*Tate hot mit alts zikh shoyn gezegnt.*
*Itst ligt er tsurik oyfn taptshan*
*un er redt tsu mir mit libn shmeykhl*
*verter umfarshtendlikhe. Ikh lig*
*shvaygik oyfn dil, un modne tseykhns*
*gibn in mayn tifenish a blik:*
*Tsankendike farbn — tate — yingl,*
*un in fayern dos yunge harts.*
*Fun dem shtiln ovntikn vinkl*
*veynt arop di fidl vays vi kvarts.*

Whiteness circles round. The landscape is a pall.
Like a swan the farm hut glides off ahead.
Father has already taken leave of all.
Now he lies back upon his planked bed
and speaks to me with a loving smile
words unfathomable. I lie
speechless on the floor, and strange signs
glance from my inward eye:
flickering colors — father — child —
and the youthful heart on fire.
In the quiet night-filled nook
the fiddle weeps, white as quartz.

אויפן בוידעם די פארבענקטע טויבן
האבן לאנג געוואָרקעט שטילערהייט.
ס׳האָט דער ווינט געחלפט דורך די שויבן.
און דער וואַלד, ווי פון אַ שווערער קייט,
אַ צערייצטער וואָלף, האָט זיך געריסן
פון די וואָרצלען — — — — — —
— — — — — — — — — —

*Oyfn boydem di farbenkte toybn*
*hobn lang gevorket shtilerheyt.*
*s'hot der vint gekheleft durkh di shoybn.*
*Un der vald, vi fun a shverer keyt,*
*a tsereytster volf, hot zikh gerisn*
*fun di vortslen — — — — — —*
*— — — — — — — — — —*

**11**

In the attic the yearning doves
have long cooed quietly.
The wind slashed through the pane.
And the forest, like a wolf maddened
by heavy chains, strained
at its roots — — — — — — —
— — — — — — — — — —

# די באַבעשי ...

די באַבעשי געװעזן איז אַ ייִדענע אַ צנועה,
אַ מײַסטער פֿון אַ קינדלערקע — אַ קינד צו יעדן פֿרילינג ...
און גרינג, און גאָר אָן װייען, פּונקט װי הינער לייגן אייער,
האָט זי געלייגט די צװילינגן — אַ צװילינג נאָך אַ צװילינג.
דרײַ פֿעטערס האָט די באַבעשי געבאָרן אױפֿן בוידעם,
צװיי פֿעטערס האָט די באַבעשי געבאָרן אױפֿן אויוון,
מײַן טאַטן האָט די באַבעשי געבאָרן אין אַ שײַער ...
און דאַן האָט זי איר מוטערטראַכט אויף אייביק צוגעשלאָסן,
די באַבעשי האָט אָפּגעשענקט פֿאַר אָרעמע די װינדעלעך,
די באַבעשי, די טײַערע, האָט אָפּגעטאָן דאָס איריקע,
איז זי אין שטוב אַרומגעגאַנגען,
װי אַ קאַטשקע צװישן הינדעלעך ...

# DI BOBESHI . . .

*Di bobeshi gevezn iz a yidene a tsnueh,*
*a mayster fun a kindlerke — a kind tsu yedn friling . . .*
*Un gring, un gor on veyen, punkt vi hiner leygn eyer,*
*hot zi geleygt di tsvilingen — a tsviling nokh a tsviling.*
*Dray feters hot di bobeshi geborn oyfn boydem,*
*tsvey feters hot di bobeshi geborn oyfn oyvn,*
*mayn tate hot di bobeshi geborn in a shayer . . .*
*Un dan hot zi ir mutertrakht oyf eybik tsugeshlosn,*
*di bobeshi hot opgeshenkt far oreme di vindelekh.*
*Di bobeshi, di tayere, hot opgeton dos irike,*
*iz zi in shtub arumgegangen,*
*vi a katshke tvishn hindelekh. . .*

# 12

## MOYSHE KULBAK

### GRANDMA

Grandma was a Jewess of modest piety,
a genius at childbearing — a child for every Spring . . .
And easily, quite without pain, a chicken laying eggs,
she laid her twins, twin after twin she'd bring.
Three uncles my Grandma bore up in the garret,
two uncles my Grandma bore upon the stove,
my Grandma bore my father in a barn . . .
And then she locked her womb forever.
Grandma gave to the poor the swaddling clothes.
Grandma, dearest one, had done her duty
and she walked about the house
a duck among the chickens.

# די באָבעשי ע"ה איז אויסגעגאַנגען . . .

אַז די באָבעשי די אלטיטשקע איז אויסגעגאַנגען,
האָבן פייגעלעך געזונגען,
ווייל מיט איר צדקה, מיט איר האַרץ דער גוטער
האָט די וועלט געקלונגען.


און אַז מען האָט די באָבעשי אַראָפּגעהויבן,
האָט אַיעדערער געשוויגן,
און אָן אַ קרעכץ האָט מען די גוטע אלטיטשקע
אויף דרערד געלאָזן ליגן.


עס איז דער זיידעניו אין שטוב אַרומגעגאַנגען —
אַ טויטער שאַרבן,
ווייל ער, דער אלטיטשקער, ער האָט איר צוגעזאָגט,
אַז ער וועט פריער שטאַרבן.


# DI BOBESHI AYEN HEY IZ OYSGEGANGEN . . .

*Az di bobeshi di altitshke iz oysgegangen,*
*hobn feygelekh gezungen,*
*vayl mit ir tsedoke, mit ir harts der guter*
*hot di velt geklungen.*

*Un az men hot di bobeshi aropgehoybn,*
*hot ayederer geshvign,*
*un on a krekhts hot men di gute altitshke*
*oyf drerd gelozn lign.*

*Es iz der zeydenyu in shtub arumgegangen —*
*a toyter sharbn,*
*vayl er, der altitshker, er hot ir tsugezogt,*
*az er vet frier shtarbn.*

# 13

## MOYSHE KULBAK

### GRANDMA, MAY SHE REST IN PEACE, DIED

When Grandma, so very old, was near death
little birds were singing.
With her charity, her generous heart
the world was ringing.

And when Grandma was carried down
no one made a sound,
and no one groaned when the good old one
was laid out upon the ground.

Grandpa roamed about the house,
a broken earthen pot,
because he, the old one, had promised her
to die first would be his lot.

און אז מען האט דעם בר-מינן אראפגעפירט אין שטעטל,
האט דער דארף געטרויערט:
„ניעמא, ניעמא יוזש סטאראי שליאמיכע",
און אויך דער פאפ וואסילי האט באדויערט...

נאר אז דער שמת האט דאס מעסרל ארויסגעצויגן
צו רייסן קריעה,
דאן האבן זיך צעשריען, נעבעך, מיינע פעטערס,
ווי די רוצחים פאר דער תליה.

Un az men hot dem bar-minon aropgefirt in shtetl,
hot der dorf getroyert:
"Nyema, nyema yuzh storoy Shloymikhe,"
un oykh der pop Vasili hot badoyert . . .

Nor az der shames hot dos meserl aroysgetsoygn
tsu raysn kriye,
dan hobn zikh tseshriyen, nebekh, mayne feters,
vi di rotskhim far der tliye.

Nyema, nyema yuzh storoy Shloymikhe: nishto, nishto
shoyn di alte shloymekhe.

**13**

And when the corpse was brought to town,
the whole village cried:
"Niema, niema yuzh storoy Shliomikhe."
And the priest Vassily sympathized. . .

But when the sexton drew his knife
to rip their mourning clothes,
only then my uncles, poor wretches, screamed
like killers at the gallows.

The Polish Niema, niema yuzh storoy Shliomikhe is
translated the old Shlome's wife is no more.

# ליבשאַפט

שלאַנקע הירשן אויף פֿאַרשנייטע בערג,
די זילבערנע הערנער פֿאַרטשעפּען די לבנה
און די לבנה איז גוט צו זיי.

מיין מאַמע היט זיי. גייט זיי נאָך פּיס־טריט.
די וועלף אין וואַלד זאָלן נישט דערניוכען.
פֿאַרלעשט זי די שפּורן אויפֿן שניי.

מיין מאַמע איז שוין זינט יאָרן טויט,
נאָר איר ליבשאַפֿט גייט אַרום אין רוים
מיט אָפֿענע אָרעמס פֿאַרן ווינט.

## LIBSHAFT

*Shlanke hirshn oyf farshneyte berg,*
*di zilberne herner fartshepen di levone*
*un di levone iz gut tsu zey.*

*Mayn mame hit zey. Geyt zey nokh fis-trit.*
*Di velf in vald zoln nisht derniukhen.*
*Farlesht zi di shpurn oyfn shney.*

*Mayn mame iz shoyn zint yorn toyt,*
*nor ir libshaft geyt arum in roym*
*mit ofene orems farn vint.*

# 14

## ITZIK MANGER

### LOVE

Tall deer upon snowy hills,
their silver horns hooked into the moon.
The moon is benevolent.

My mother guards them. Follows them on foot.
Forest wolves must not find their spoor.
She blows from the snow their scent.

My mother has been dead for years,
but her love roams through space
with arms open to the wind.

זי שלעפֿערט איין דעם אומרו פֿון די שטראָזן,
שפּרעכט אָפּ אַ „גוט אויג" די קלײנע האָזן
און דאָס מינדסטע ווערימל רופֿט זי „קינד".

די ליבשאַפֿט לאָזט זי נישט אין קבֿר רוען.

אָט עפֿנט זי די תּחינה פֿאַר די שטערן
און זאָגט און זאָגט, אַז גאָט זאָל זי דערהערן.

אין מײן חלום לײַכטן אירע טרערן...

*Zi shlefert ayn dem umru fun di shtrozn,*
*shprekht op a "gut oyg" di kleyne hozn*
*un dos mindste veriml ruft zi "kind."*

*Di libshaft lozt zi nisht in keyver ruen.*

*Ot efnt zi di tkhine far di shtern*
*un zogt un zogt, az got zol zi derhern.*

*In mayn kholem laykhtn ire trern...*

**14**

She lulls the unrest of the streets to sleep,
conjures up a "good eye" the little hares can keep,
and the least worm she calls "child."

Her love does not let her rest in her grave.

Here she opens her prayer book for the stars
and prays and prays, that God may hear.

In my dream gleams her tear.

# די מאמע

די מאמע אין גרינעם סוועדער גייט איבערן גאַס און גייט.
אלול הוידעט זיך דער ווינט,
טבת שנייט,
זון איבער די שויבן פּסח רינט.
דער גרינער סוועדער גייט איבערן גאַס און גייט
שוין זומערן,
שוין ווינטערן,
שוין וויפל צייט —
די גאַסן שווימען אין דער לאַנג און אין דער קרים,
דער הימל הוידעט זיך אַזוי ווי אַ האַמאַק,
און אַלע גאַסן,
אַלע פירן צום פּאַוויאַק.

# DI MAME

*Di mame in grinem sveder geyt ibern gas un geyt.*
*Eylul hoydet zikh der vint,*
*Teyves shneyt,*
*zun iber di shoybn Peysakh rint.*
*Der griner sveder geyt ibern gas un geyt*
*shoyn zumern,*
*shoyn vintern,*
*shoyn viful tsayt —*
*di gasn shvimen in der lang un in der krim,*
*der himl hoydet zikh azoy vi a hamak,*
*un ale gasn,*
*ale firn tsum Paviak.*

# 15

# KADIE MOLODOWSKY

## THE MOTHER

The green-sweatered mother walks and walks the street.
In Elul the wind swings,
in Tebet it snows,
at Passover sun floods the windows.
The green sweater walks and walks the street
through summers,
through winters —
such a long time.
The streets slither lengthwise or all awry,
the sky swings like a hammock,
and all streets,
all lead to the Paviak.

דאָרט ווי אַ וואונד אַ קאַמער בריט,
אַ קאַמער וויגט זיך טאָג און נאַכט;
אונטער די גרויע ווענט אַ טאָכטער זיצט פֿאַרמאַכט,
פֿאַרשלאָסן,
שטיל,
מיט אויפֿגעלייגטע הענט,
מיט שאַרפֿן הערן,
און זעגט די קראַטן מיטן בליק
און ציילט די שטערן.
אַרום די שטילקייט קלינגט,
עס בלענדט די ליידיקייט מיט ווייסע שפּיזן.
—  —  —  —  —  —  —  —  —
—  —  —  —  —  —  —  —  —

Dort vi a vund a kamer brit,
a kamer vigt zikh tog un nakht;
unter di groye vent a tokhter zitst farmakht,
farshlosn,
shtil,
mit oyfgeleygte hent,
mit sharfn hern,
un zegt di kratn mitn blik
un tseylt di shtern.
Arum di shtilkayt klingt,
es blendt di leydikayt mit vayse shpizn.
—  —  —  —  —  —  —  —  —
—  —  —  —  —  —  —  —  —

**15**

There a prison burns like a wound,
a prison rocks through days and nights;
a daughter sits shut behind those gray heights,
locked in,
mute,
with folded hands,
with sharpened ears,
and saws the gratings with her glance
and counts the stars.
Round and round the silence rings,
emptiness dazzles with whitened spears.
— — — — — — — — — — —
— — — — — — — — — —

דער גרינער סוועדער גייט איבערן גאס און גייט.
אלול איז נישט נאס,
און טבת איז נישט קאלט,
און פסח איז קיין יום-טוב נישט.

דער הימל הוידעט זיך אזוי ווי א האמאק,
און אלע גאסן,
אלע פירן צום פאוויאק.

*Der griner sveder geyt ibern gas un geyt.*
*Eylul iz nisht nas,*
*un Teyves iz nisht kalt,*
*un Peysakh iz kayn yom-tov nisht.*

*Der himl hoydet zikh azoy vi a hamak,*
*un ale gasn,*
*ale firn tsum Paviak.*

**15**

The green sweater walks and walks the street.
Elul is not wet,
and Tebet is not cold,
and Passover no holiday.

The sky swings like a hammock,
and all streets,
all lead to the Paviak.

Elul: twelfth month of the Jewish calendar (August September).
Tebet: fourth month of the Jewish calendar (December-January).
Passover: spring holiday in memory of the Exodus from Egypt.
Paviak: prison on Pavia Street in Warsaw's East Side that held
political prisoners.

## אײנזאַם

קיינער ווייסט נישט, וואָס איך זאָג,
קיינער ווייסט נישט, וואָס איך וויל —
זיבן מייזלעך מיט אַ מויז
שלאָפֿן אויפֿן דיל.

זיבן מייזלעך מיט אַ מויז
זענען, דוכט זיך, אַכט —
טו איך אָן דעם קאַפּעלוש
און זאָג: „אַ גוטע נאַכט".

טו איך אָן דעם קאַפּעלוש
און איך לאָז זיך גיין.
וואו זשע גייט מען שפּעט ביינאַכט
אייניקער אַליין?

## AYNZAM

*Keyner veyst nisht, vos ikh zog,*
*keyner veyst nisht, vos ikh vil —*
*zibn mayzlekh mit a moyz*
*shlofn oyfn dil.*

*Zibn mayzlekh mit a moyz*
*zenen, dukht zikh, akht —*
*tu ikh on dem kapelush*
*un zog: "A gute nakht."*

*Tu ikh on dem kapelush*
*un ikh loz zikh geyn.*
*Vu zhe geyt men shpet baynakht*
*eyniker aleyn?*

# 16

# ITZIK MANGER

## ALONE

No one knows what it is I say,
no one knows what I wish for —
seven mouselets and a mouse
are sleeping on the floor.

Seven mouselets and a mouse
make, I think, eight —
so I put my hat upon my head
and say: Good night.

I put my hat upon my head
and I am gone.
Where does one go late at night
all, all alone?

שטייט אַ שענק אין מיטן מאַרק,
ווינקט צו מיר: „דו יאָלד!
כ'האָב אַ פעסעלע מיט וויין,
אַ פעסעלע מיט גאָלד".

עפֿן שנעל איך אויף די טיר
און איך פֿאַל אַריין:
„אַ גוט יום־טוב אַלע אייך,
ווער איר זאָלט ניט זיין!"

קיינער ווייסט נישט, וואָס איך זאָג,
קיינער ווייסט נישט, וואָס איך וויל —
צוויי שיכורים מיט אַ פֿלאַש
שלאָפֿן אויפֿן דיל.

*Shteyt a shenk in mitn mark,*
*vinkt tsu mir: "Du yold!*
*Kh'hob a fesele mit vayn,*
*a fesele mit gold."*

*Efn shnel ikh oyf di tir*
*un ikh fal arayn:*
*"A gut yom-tov ale aykh,*
*ver ir zolt nisht zayn!"*

*Keyner veyst nisht, vos ikh zog,*
*keyner veyst nisht, vos ikh vil —*
*tsvey shikurim mit a flash*
*shlofn oyfn dil.*

**16**

An inn stands in the square,
winks to me: "You fool!
I have a cask of wine,
a small cask of gold."

Quickly I open the door,
make my entry:
"Good holiday to all of you,
whoever you may be."

No one knows what it is I say,
no one knows what I wish for —
two drunkards with a flask
are sleeping on the floor.

צוויי שכורים מיט אַ פּלאַש
זענען, דוכט זיך, דריי.
זיין אַ פערטער דאָ אין שפּיל
לוינט זיך? — נישט כּדאי.

טו איך אָן דעם קאַפּעלוש
און איך לאָז זיך גיין.
וואָזשע גייט מען שפּעט ביינאַכט
אייניקער אַליין?

*Tsvey shikurim mit a flash*
*zenen, dukht zikh, dray.*
*Zayn a ferter do in shpil*
*loynt zikh? — Nisht keday.*

*Tu ikh on dem kapelush*
*un ikh loz zikh geyn.*
*Vuzhe geyt men shpet baynakht*
*eyniker aleyn?*

**16**

Two drunkards with a flask
make, I think, three.
Does it pay to be fourth
in this game — not for me.

So I put my hat upon my head
and I am gone.
Where does one go late at night,
all, all alone?

# ביאגראפיע

ס'טרויערן אויף אין מיר זיננגנדיקע ערטער,
זיי שטעלן זיך אויס און ווערן ווערטער
פון פארצייכנטע מעמואַרן.
שוואַרץ אויף ווייס פאַרשריבן,
מיט אַ זיכרון אַ ליכט-געטונקטן.
כ'קען זיך גאָרניט נאַרן.

אַ לעבן צוזאַמענגעשטעלט פון שטיקער געאָגראַפיע.
גאַסן און שטיבער,
לאָמפן און בעטן,
פּנימער און סילועטן
זיינען די קאָמאַס און פּונקטן
פון מיין ביאַגראַפיע.

## BIOGRAFIYE

S'troyern oyf in mir zingendike erter,
zey shteln zikh oys un vern verter
fun fartseykhnte memuarn.
Shvarts oyf vays farshribn,
mit a zikorun a likht-getunktn.
Kh'ken zikh gornit narn.

A lebn tsuzamengeshtelt fun shtiker geografiye.
Gasn un shtiber,
lompn un betn,
penemer un siluetn
zaynen di komes un punktn
fun mayn biografiye.

# 17

# J. GLATSTEIN

## BIOGRAPHY

Singing places surge in me, sorrow-stirred;
they arrange themselves and become the words
of recorded memories,
written in black on white
by a memory dipped in light.
I can't even fool myself.

A life pieced together from scraps of geography.
Streets and houses,
lamps and beds,
faces and silhouettes
are the commas and periods
of my biography.

HOW BLESSED AM I
AND HOW BLESSED AND BLESSED

The miracle rabbi of the eighteenth century, Yisroel Balshemtov (1700–1760), leader of the school of celebrating God's glory with joy and song and dance, is a natural focus for the poet's admiration. Both Landau and Manger show the Balshem's appeal (he was the founder of Hasidism, a central strain in Jewish living and theology). Mani Leib, so many of whose poems speculated upon the coming of a messiah, describes the ancient legend of the prophet Elijah's continual solicitude for his people. (At Passover a beaker of wine is always set for him, and the door left open for his arrival.) Itzik Manger has written several cycles of poems based on Biblical tales. Their contemporary idiom and freshness set them apart from the usual retelling of these stories — Naomi and her daughters-in-law are solidly placed in a small village context, and the daughters receive letters from their village priests exhorting them to return home now that their Jewish husbands are dead. Manger's Hagar poems work in the same way. When Hagar arrives at the railway station (Abraham has quarreled over the fare with the driver taking her there), she holds Ishmael and muses, servant-girl fashion, upon the arbitrariness of the Patriarchs. "The Binding of Isaac" is one of the best of an astonishingly large number of Yiddish poems that are concerned with Christianity and its relation to Judaism. Yehoash once wrote, in a poem called "Angelus," of "the still consolation of a God not mine." Einhorn too is concerned with the messianic hope, as is Glatstein in his ironical backward glance in "The Messenger" and "The Shining Fool."

# אין דער הייליקער בעל שם טוב . . .

איז דער הייליקער בעל שם טוב אין פעלד ארומגעגאנגען,
באגינען אין פעלד אינם קאלטן געגאנגען.
קאלט און פראסטיק האבן געבלאזן די ווינטן,
עם האבן פון צפון געבלאזן די ווינטן,
אז ס'האבן גענומען אים פרירן די גלידער;
און ס'האט מיט פארפראָרענע גלידער,
דער הייליקער בעל שם טוב געעפנט די לעפצן
און האט אפן קול זיך צעזונגען.
אזוי האבן זיינע געעפנטע לעפצן
געזונגען, געזונגען, געזונגען:
„אז וואויל איז צו דעם, וואָס האָט זוכה געווען
„דיין ווינט זאָל אמאל אים באַרירן,
„אז וואויל איז צו מיר, וואָס כ'האָב זוכה געווען,
„פון קעלטן פון דיינע צו פרירן;
„אז וואויל איז צו מיר און אז וואויל איז און וואויל,
„אז וואויל איז און וואויל איז און וואויל".


# IZ DER HEYLIKER BALSHEMTOV . . .

*Iz der heyliker Balshemtov in feld arumgegangen,*
*baginen in feld inm kaltn gegangen.*
*Es hobn fun tsofn geblozn di vintn,*
*kalt un frostik hobn geblozn di vintn,*
*az s'hobn genumen im frirn di glider;*
*un s'hot mit farfrorene glider,*
*der heyliker Balshemtov geëfnt di leftsn*
*un hot afn kol zikh tsezungen.*
*Azoy hobn zayne geëfnte leftsn*
*gezungen, gezungen, gezungen:*
*"Az voyl iz tsu dem, vos hot zoykhe geven*
*dayn vint zol amol im barirn,*
*az voyl is tsu mir, vos kh'hob zoykhe geven*
*fun keltn fun dayne tsu frirn;*
*az voyl iz tsu mir un az voyl iz un voyl,*
*az voyl iz un voyl iz un voyl."*

# 18

## ZISHA LANDAU

### THE HOLY BALSHEMTOV

The holy Balshemtov walked through the fields,
walked at dawn through the cold fields.
From the north the winds were blowing,
cold and frosted the winds were blowing,
and the cold began to freeze his limbs,
and with frozen limbs
the holy Balshemtov opened his lips
and aloud he began his singing.
Thus were his opened lips
singing, singing, singing:
"How blessed is he that has been favored
once to be touched by Your wind.
How blessed am I that I have been favored
to freeze in the cold of Your wind;
how blessèd am I and how blessèd and blessed,
how blessèd and blessèd and blessed."

און דורשטיק די פּראָסטיקע לופט אַלץ געטרונקען
און ווידער אין טיפע מחשבות פֿאַרזונקען.

און ביסלעכווייז איז אינם הימל אַרויס
אַ זון אַזוי פֿלאַמיק און גרויס,
אַז ווי אין גיהנום געוואָרן איז הייס,
פֿון פּנים גערונען האָט טראָפּנווייז שווייס
און ס׳האָט אינם ברענענדן פֿעלד
קיין ווינטל צומאָל ניט געוויעט.
נאָר פּלוצים זיך האָט דורכן ברענענדן פֿעלד,
דאָס קול פֿון בעל שם טוב צעשפּרייט;
דאָס האָט דער בעל שם טוב געזונגען,

*Un durshtik di frostike luft alts getrunken*
*un vider in tife makhshoves farzunken.*

*Un bislekhvayz iz inm himl aroys*
*a zun azoy flamik un groys,*
*az vi in gehenim gevorn iz heys,*
*fun ponim gerunen hot tropnvayz shveys*
*un s'hot inm brenendn feld*
*kayn vintl tsumol nit geveyt.*
*Nor plutsim zikh hot durkhn brenendn feld*
*dos kol fun Balshemtov tseshpreyt;*
*dos hot der Balshemtov gezungen,*

And the frosty air he thirstily drank
and once more into deep meditation sank.

And little by little in the sky emerged
a sun so flaming and large
that it became Gehenna-hot.
From his face the sweat drops fell
and in the burning field
no breeze blew at all.
But suddenly over the burning field
the Balshemtov spread his call;
thus the Balshemtov was singing,

א לויב דעם באַשעפֿער געזונגען:

„פֿאַר קעלטן און היצן, פֿאַר זון און פֿאַר רעגן,

„פֿאַר טאָג און פֿאַר נאַכט, דיר אַ לויב!

„פֿאַר אַלץ, וואָס דו שיקסט דעם מענטשן אַנטקעגן,

„אַ לויב דיר, אַ לויב דיר, אַ לויב!

„און וואָויל איז צו מיר, וואָס איך ווער איצט פֿאַרברענט,

„פֿון פֿייערן דיינע פֿאַרברענט.

„און אויב איך בין זוכֿה, און דו האָסט באַשערט,

„צו פֿאַלן פֿון דורשטיקייט איצט אַף דיין ערד,

„ווי וואָויל איז צו מיר און ווי וואָויל איז און וואָויל

„און וואָויל איז און וואָויל איז און וואָויל".

a loyb dem bashefer gezungen:
"Far keltn un hitsn, far zun un far regn,
far tog un far nakht, dir a loyb!
Far alts, vos du shikst dem mentshn antkegn,
a loyb dir, a loyb dir, a loyb!
Un voyl iz tsu mir, vos ikh ver itst farbrent,
fun fayern dayne farbrent.
Un oyb ikh bin zoykhe, un du host bashert
tsu faln fun durshtikayt itst af dayn erd,
vi voyl iz tsu mir un vi voyl iz un voyl
un voyl iz un voyl iz un voyl."

praise to the Creator singing:
"For cold and for heat, for sun and for rain,
for day and for night, be You praised.
For all that You send toward each man
praised be You, praised be You, praised,
and blessed am I that I am now burning,
in Your fires burning.
And if I am favored, and You have fated
that I fall to Your earth, my thirst unsated,
how blessèd am I and how blessèd and blessed
and blessèd and blessèd and blessed."

Balshemtov: literally "Master of the Good Name," epithet of the founder
of the Hasidic sect, which practises service to God through joy. The Balshem
is noted in legend as a "wonder rabbi."

# סאַנקט בעש״ט

זיצט דער בעל שם קעגן מיטן־נאַכט
אין זײן חדר מיוחד און ער טראַכט:
"די נאַכט איז הייליק, טיף און שײן,
אַז אַפילו דער מענטש, וואָס גייט אַליין
באָרוועס איבער אַ פרעמדן לאַנד,
פילט איבער זיך גאָט׳ס בלאָע האַנט".

ער הויבט זיך אויף און בלײבט פלוצים שטיין:
אין פענצטער ציטערט אַ דין געוויין.
ווער וויינט בײנאַכט, ווער וויינט אַצינד,
ווען ס׳שלאָפט דער פויגל און ס׳שלאָפט דער ווינט,
ווען ס׳שלאָפט די כאַטע, און ס׳שלאָפט דער וואַלד?
ווער טרײבט פון זײן חלום אַוועק דאָס גאָלד?
"הער — זאָגט ער צום פרעמדן געוויין געוועענדט —
קום און ווער אַנטשלאָפן אויף מײנע הענט".

*SANKT BES"T*

*Zitst der Balshem kegn mitn-nakht*
*in zayn kheyder meyukhed un er trakht:*
*"Di nakht iz heylik, tif un sheyn,*
*az afile der mentsh, vos geyt aleyn*
*borves iber a fremdn land,*
*filt iber zikh gots bloe hant."*

*Er hoybt zikh oyf un blaybt plutsim shteyn:*
*In fenster tstitert a din geveyn.*
*Ver veynt baynakht, ver veynt atsind,*
*ven s'shloft der foygl un s'shloft der vint,*
*ven s'shloft di khate, un s'shloft der vald?*
*Ver traybt fun zayn kholem avek dos gold?*
*"Her — zogt er tsum fremdn geveyn gevendt —*
*kum un ver antshlofn oyf mayne hent."*

# 19

# ITZIK MANGER

## SAINT BALSHEMTOV

In the middle of the night the Balshem rests
in his lonely room and reflects:
"The night is so holy, lovely, and deep,
that even the man who walks alone,
barefoot, over an alien land,
feels overhead God's blue hand."

He arises and remains stock-still.
A thin wail quakes at his windowsill.
Who weeps at night? Who now weeps,
when the bird sleeps and the wind sleeps?
When the hut sleeps and the wood sleeps?
Who drives the gold away from his dream?
"Listen," the strange wail he commands.
"Come and fall asleep upon my hands."

נאָר ס'ציטערט דאָס געוויין ווי אַ פֿידל דין,
דין ווי דאָס שפּינגעוועב פֿון אַ שפּין,
דין ווי די גסיסה פֿון אַ קינד,
וואָס פֿאַרוואַרפֿט דאָס קעפּל אויפֿן ווינט.

עפֿנט דער בעל שם די טיר און גייט
געוואָר צו ווערן, ווער ס'שטערט די פֿרייד,
די פֿרייד און דעם חלום פֿון אַ וועלט.
אָט דרימלט די שטאָט, אָט דרימלט דער טײַך.
אָט דרימלט דאָס פֿעלד.
ווער-זשע וויינט אַצינד,
ווען ס'שלאָפֿט דער פֿויגל און ס'שלאָפֿט דער ווינט,
ווען ס'שלאָפֿט די כאַטע און ס'שלאָפֿט דער וואַלד?
ווער טרײַבט פֿון זיין חלום אַוועק דאָס גאָלד?
„הער — זאָגט ער צום פֿרעמדן געוויין געוועגדט —
קום און ווער אַנטשלאָפֿן אויף מײַנע הענט".

Nor s'tsitert dos geveyn vi a fidl din,
din vi dos shpingeveb fun a shpin,
din vi di gsise fun a kind,
vos farvarft dos kepl oyfn vint.

Efnt der Balshem di tir un geyt,
gevor tsu vern, ver s'shtert di freyd,
di freyd un dem kholem fun a velt.
Ot drimlt di shtot, ot drimlt der taykh.
Ot drimlt dos feld.
Ver — zhe veynt atsind,
ven s'shloft der foygl un s'shloft der vint,
ven s'shloft di khate, un s'shloft der vald?
Ver traybt fun zayn kholem avek dos gold?
"Her — zogt er tsum fremdn geveyn gevendt —
kum un ver antshlofn oyf mayne hent."

But the wail trembles like a fiddle so thin,
thin as the spiderweb spiders spin,
as the death-bed sob of a child is thin
that tosses its little head in the wind.

The Balshem opens the door and goes
to discover who troubles the joy,
the joy and the dream of a world.
Here dreams the town. Here dreams the stream.
Here dreams the field.
Who then now weeps,
when the bird sleeps and the wind sleeps?
When the hut sleeps and the wood sleeps?
Who drives the gold away from his dream?
"Listen!" the strange wail he commands.
"Come and fall asleep upon my hands."

נאָר ס׳ציטערט דאָס געוויין ווי אַ פֿידל דין,
דין ווי דאָס שפּינגעוועב פֿון אַ שפּין,
דין ווי די גסיסה פֿון אַ קינד,
וואָס פֿאַרוואַרפֿט דאָס קעפּל אויפֿן ווינט.

הויבט דער בעל שם די אויגן אויף,
די ליכטיקע אויגן צום הימל אַרויף,
זעט ער אַ גראָע כמאַרע וואָס ליגט
איבער אַ שטערן, וואָס ווערט צעדריקט.
בלייבט דער בעל שם אַ רגע שטיין
און הערט זיך צו צום זילבערנעם געוויין.

*Nor s'tsitert dos geveyn vi a fidl din,*
*din vi dos shpingeveb fun a shpin,*
*din vi di gsise fun a kind,*
*vos farvarft dos kepl oyfn vint.*

*Hoybt der Balshem di oygn oyf,*
*di likhtike oygn tsum himl aroyf,*
*zet er a groe khmare vos ligt*
*iber a shtern, vos vert tsedrikt.*
*Blaybt der Balshem a rege shteyn*
*un hert zikh tsu tsum zilbernem geveyn.*

But the wail trembles like a fiddle so thin,
thin as the spiderweb spiders spin,
as the death-bed sob of a child is thin
that tosses its little head in the wind.

The Balshem lifts up his eyes —
lifts them glowing to the skies.
He sees a grey cloud lying brushed
over a star being crushed.
The Balshem stands for a moment there,
listens to the silvered despair.

דערנאָך הויבט ער אויף די ליכטיקע האַנט,
צום הימל אַרויף די ליכטיקע האַנט,
און וישט די גראָע כמאַרע אַוועק.
פלאַטערט דער שטערן באַפרײַט פון שרעק,
פלאַטערט און שימערט, בליצט און קלינגט
אַדורך דער לופט, ווי גינגאָלד קלינגט.
שמייכלט דער בעל שם: „דו שייגעץ, דו!
האָסט אויפגעטרייסלט אַ וועלט פון רו".


מיט שטילע טריט גייט ער דאַן אַהיים,
אַהיים צו זײַן כאַטע פון ציגל און ליים,
און זעצט זיך אַנידער אויפן שוועל,
און וואַרט אויפן ערשטן פויגל-טרעל,
און וואַרט אויפן ערשטן טראָפן זון.
אויפן ערשטן גאָלדענעם טראָפן זון.
און אײדער דער טאָג האָט אויפגעטאָגט,
האָט ער שטיל צו זיך אַלײן געזאָגט:




*Dernokh heybt er oyf di likhtike hant,*
*tsum himl aroyf di likhtike hant,*
*un visht di groe khmare avek.*
*Flatert der shtern bafrayt fun shrek,*
*flatert un shimert, blitst un klingt*
*adurkh der luft, vi gingold klingt.*
*Shmeykhlt der Balshem: "Du sheygets, du.*
*Host oyfgetreyslt a velt fun ru."*

*Mit shtile trit geyt er dan aheym,*
*aheym tsu zayn khate fun tsigl un leym,*
*un zetst zikh anider oyfn shvel,*
*un vart oyfn ershtn foygl-trel,*
*un vart oyfn ershtn tropn zun.*
*Oyfn ershtn goldenem tropn zun.*
*Un eyder der tog hot oyfgetogt,*
*hot er shtil tsu zikh aleyn gezogt:*

**19**

Then he raises his glowing hand —
raises to the sky his glowing hand,
and wipes the grey cloud away.
The star flutters freed from fear,
flutters and shimmers, sparkles and rings
through the air, as fine gold rings.
The Balshem smiles: "You rascal, you.
A world from its rest you have shaken askew."

Then with soft steps he returns home,
home to his hut of brick and of loam,
and sits down upon his doorsill
and waits for the first bird trill
and waits for the first drop of sun,
for the first golden drop of sun.
And before the day rose overhead,
softly to himself he said:

„דאָס געוויין פֿון אַ ווערמל און פֿון אַ גראָז,
דאָס געוויין פֿון אַ שטערנדל און פֿון אַ האָז
קען טרייסלען און צעטרייסלען אַ וועלט פֿון רו
באַהיט און באַשיץ זיי, טאַטע דו!"

און אַ ליכטיקער טראָפֿן פֿאַלט אויף זיין האַנט
און קייקלט זיך אַראָפּ איבער זיין געוואַנט.

"Dos geveyn fun a vereml un fun a groz,
dos geveyn fun a shterndl un fun a hoz
ken treyslen un tsetreyslen a velt fun ru
Bahit un bashits zey, tate du!"

Un a likhtiker tropn falt oyf zayn hant
un kayklt zikh arop iber zayn gevant.

**19**

"The wail of a worm and of a grass,
the wail of a star and of a hare
can shake and shake out a world from its rest —
guard and protect them, Father up there."

Over his hands a gleaming drop flows
and rolls downward upon his clothes.

# דער ליכטיקער נאר

שױן לאַנג נישט געזען
דעם ליכטיקן נאַר,
װאָס באַצװינגט װי אַ האַר
די שטומע, פֿאַרפֿינצטערטע חכמים.
שױן לאַנג נישט געזען
דעם פֿאַרגלױבטן און געבענטשטן תם.

## DER LIKHTIKER NAR

*Shoyn lang nisht gezen*
*dem likhtikn nar,*
*vos batsvingt vi a har*
*di shtume, farfintsterte khakhomim.*
*Shoyn lang nisht gezen*
*dem fargloybtn un gebentshtn tam.*

# 20

## J. GLATSTEIN

## THE SHINING FOOL

For a long time we have not seen
the shining fool
who rules like a lord
the mute, darkened wise men.
For a long time we have not seen
the believing and blessed fool.

נאָר אָט איז ער אַרױס פֿון אונדזער שטאַם
אַ דורכגעברענטער סאַלאַמאַנדער.
דער הײליקער װאָגלער
איז געקומען צו אונדז
פֿון אַ װײטן געפּײניקטן װאַנדער,
אַראָפּגעטרײסלט דעם נע־ונדיקן שטױב
און געזונגען מיט דבֿקות
אָ, אני מאמין, איך גלױב!
איך גלױב און איך גלױב.


הײ, װער ביסטו, דו?
װער איז געקומען שטערן
פֿון חכמים די פֿינצטערע רו?
װער איז געקומען זײַען גלױביקע קערנער?
מיטאַמאָל האָבן אַלע דערזען,
װי ס׳לײַכטן אױף זײַן קאָפּ,
משה׳ס פֿאַרנאַרישטע, גלױביקע,
שטראַלנדיקע הערנער.


*Nor ot iz er aroys fun undzer shtam*
*a durkhgebrenter salamander.*
*Der heyliker vogler*
*iz gekumen tsu undz*
*fun a vaytn gepayniktn vander,*
*aropgetreyslt dem na-venandikn shtoyb*
*un gezungen mit dveykes*
*o, ani mamin, ikh gloyb!*
*Ikh gloyb un ikh gloyb.*

*Hey, ver bistu, du?*
*Ver iz gekumen shtern*
*fun khakhomim di fintstere ru?*
*Ver iz gekumen zeyen gloybike kerner?*
*Mitamol hobn ale derzen,*
*vi s'laykhtn oyf zayn kop,*
*Moyshe's farnarishte, gloybike,*
*shtralndike herner.*

But lo he came out of our race
a charred salamander.
The holy wanderer
came to us
from a distant painful wonder,
shook off the wander dust
and sang with ecstasy
o, ani mamin, I believe!
I believe and I believe.

Hey, who are you, you?
Who has come to disturb
the dark repose of wise men?
Who has come to sow believing seeds?
Suddenly everybody saw
gleaming on his head
Moses' foolish, credulous
starlike horns.

# אליהו אין בית-מדרש

יידן זיצן אין בית-מדרש, לערנען תורה אויף אַ קול.
און אַ ייד, וואָס קען ניט לערנען, זיצט און האָרכט ווי אַלעמאָל.

אויפן טיש אַ ליכטל רויכערט, וויגט די שאָטנס אויף די ווענט,
לויכט אויף אַלטע געלע ספרים, אויף די אַלטע בערד און הענט.

און אין דרויסן דרייען ווינטן, דרייען שניי און טויטע קעלט.
נאָר די יידן לערנען תורה — רוען אין אַן אַנדער וועלט.

עפנט זיך די טיר פון פּאָליש. ווי אַ בעטלער, אין דער שטיל
שאַרט אַריין זיך אליהו, לייגט זיין טאָרבע אויפ'ן דיל.

זעצט זיך ביי דעם אַלטן אויוון, וואַרעמט זיך די קאַלטע פיס,
הערט זיך צו ווי יידן לערנען, און זיין פנים שמייכלט זיס:

# ELYOHU IN BES-MEDRESH

*Yidn zitsn in bes-medresh, lernen toyre oyf a kol.*
*Un a yid, vos ken nit lernen, zitst un horkht vi alemol.*

*Oyfn tish a likhtl roykhert, vigt di shotns oyf di vent,*
*loykkht oyf alte gele sforem, oyf di alte berd un hent.*

*Un in droysn dreyen vintn, dreyen shney un toyte kelt.*
*Nor di yidn lernen toyre — ruen in an ander velt.*

*Efnt zikh der tir fun polish. Vi a betler, in der shtil*
*shart arayn zikh Elyohu, leygt zayn torbe oyf'n dil.*

*Zetst zikh bay dem altn oyvn, varemt zikh di kalte fis,*
*hert zikh tsu vi yidn lernen, un zayn ponem shmeykhlt zis:*

# 21

## MANI LEIB

## ELIJAH IN THE HOUSE OF STUDY

Jews sit in the House of Study, learn Torah, voices raised.
And a Jew, who cannot learn, sits and listens as always.

A light smokes on the table, rocks shadows on the walls;
on old yellowed books, on old beards and hands light falls.

And outside winds are swirling, snow and dead cold are
    swirled.
But the Jews study Torah — resting in another world.

Like a beggar, in the silence, opening the door,
Elijah sidles in, lays his pack upon the floor.

Sits down by the ancient stove to warm his cold feet,
listens to the Jews at study with a smile so sweet:

— לערנט, לערנט, פרומע ייִדן, תּורה איז די לוין אַליין . . .
פּלוצלונג שטעלט ער אָן אַן אויער און פֿאַרנעמט אַ שטיל געוויין.

ניט קיין חיה וויינט אין דרויסן — אין יסורים און אין זינד
ווײַט פֿאַר מײַלן אין אַ שטיבל וויינט אַ פֿרוי, וואָס גייט צו-קינד.

שאַרט ער זיך אַוועק פֿון אויוון, נעמט זיין טאָרבע פֿונ'ם דיל,
שטיל ווי ער איז אָנגעקומען, ווערט ער נעלם אין דער שטיל.

מיט דער טאָרבע אויף דער פּלייצע לאָזט זיך אליהו גיין,
און אין שניי און אין די ווינטן גייט ער נאָך דאָס שטיל געוויין.

— Lernt, lernt, frume yidn, toyre iz di loyn aleyn . . .
Plutslung shtelt er on an oyer un farnemt a shtil geveyn.

Nit kayn khaye veynt in droysn — in yesurem un in zind
vayt far mayln in a shtibl veynt a froy, vos geyt tsu-kind.

Shart er zikh avek fun oyvn, nemt zayn torbe fun'm dil,
shtil vi er iz ongekumen, vert er nelem in der shtil.

Mit der torbe oyf der pleytse lozt zikh Elyohu geyn,
un in shney un in di vintn geyt er nokh dos shtil geveyn.

**21**

— Study, study, pious Jews, Torah is its own reward . . .
Suddenly he cocks his ear; a quiet sob is heard.

No animal weeps outside — in agony and in sin,
in a faraway hut a woman weeps at her lying-in.

He slips away from the stove, takes up his pack from the
      floor,
silently as he arrived, so silently is seen no more.

Elijah sets forth with his burden on his back,
through snows and through winds on the quiet sob's track.

קומט ער צו אן אָרים שטיבל. אין יסורים און אין זינד,
אָן אַ היטער, אָן אַ טרייסטער גייט אַ יונגע פרוי צו-קינד.

גייט ער צו די פרעמדע שטיבער — ווי אַ פּאַסטוך רופט די שאַף;
קלאַפּט ער אין די פרעמדע פענצטער, וועקט די ווייבער פון'ם שלאָף.

און די ווייבער פון די שטיבער אין דער פינצטער נעמען גיין,
טראָגן טרייסט צו יענעם שטיבל, איינצושטילן דאָס געוויין.

און אין דרויסן דרייען ווינטן, דרייען שניי און טויטע קעלט.
און די יידן לערנען תורה, רוען אין אַן אנדער וועלט.

*Kumt er tsu an orim shtibl. In yesurem un in zind,*
*on a hiter, on a treyster geyt a yunge froy tsu-kind.*

*Geyt er tsu di fremde shtiber — vi a pastukh ruft di shof;*
*klapt er in di fremde fentster, vekt di vayber fun'm shlof.*

*Un di vayber fun di shtiber in der fintster nemen geyn,*
*trogn treyst tsu yenem shtibl, ayntsushtiln dos geveyn.*

*Un in droysn dreyen vintn, dreyen shney un toyte kelt.*
*Un di yidn lernen toyre, ruen in an ander velt.*

**21**

He comes to an impoverished cottage. In agony and in sin,
without protector, without consoler, a young woman is
    lying-in.

He goes to strange houses, like a shepherd calling sheep;
knocks at strange windows, rouses women from their sleep.

And in the darkness from their houses the women come out,
carrying comfort to that cottage, hush and still the shout.

And outside winds are swirling, snow and dead cold are
    swirled.
And the Jews study Torah, resting in another world.

די באַלאַדע פון דעם הייליקן אָוונט-ברויט

וואָלקן שטורעמט איבער וואָלקן. שטורעמווינט.
דורכן טונקעלן פענסטער קוקט אַרויס אַ קינד.

טראָפּ, טראָפּ. שווערע טראָפּנס קלאַפּן אויפן דאַך:
"זע, טאַטע, אורחים קומען מיטן שליאַך".

דער יונגער קאָוואַל עפנט ברייט די טיר:
"גוטן אָוונט, אורחים, קומט אַריין צו מיר.

אַ ווינקל איז פאַראַן. דער טיש געגרייט.
נעמט אָן פאַר ליב אונזער אָרעם ברויט".

*DI BALADE FUN DEM HEYLIKN*
*OVNT-BROYT*

*Volkn shturemt iber volkn. Shturemvint.*
*Durkhn tunkeln fenster kukt aroys a kind.*

*Trop, trop. Shvere tropns klapn oyfn dakh:*
*"Ze, tate, orkhim kumen mitn shliakh."*

*Der yunger koval efnt breyt di tir:*
*"Gutn ovent, orkhim, kumt arayn tsu mir.*

*A vinkl iz faran. Der tish gegreyt.*
*Nemt on far lib unzer orem broyt."*

# 22

## ITZIK MANGER

## THE BALLAD OF THE HOLY EVENING BREAD

Cloud storming over cloud. Winds and rain.
A child looks out through a darkened pane.

Drop, drop. On the roof heavy drops beat:
"See, Father, strangers come down the street."

The young blacksmith opens his door wide:
"Good evening, strangers, come inside.

There is room. The table is spread.
Please share with love our poor bread."

האָט איינע, ... ין צימער, אַ רויכיק לעמפּל ברענט,
און דער צוווייט... ... וויגן זיך אויף וועגט.

האָט דער בעל... ... ווינקל אַ ליכטיק קינדער-ראָד
און געהאָט שו... ...רצײלט פֿון גאָט'ס גענאָד:

האָלב טונקל ... ...טלער געגאַנגען אַ טאָג מיט אַ נאַכט.
ניין אורחים ב... ..., דער טויער פֿאַרמאַכט.

נאָר ס'שטייט דע... ...עגעבן דאָס רינגל אַ דרײַ,
און איבער זײַן ק... ...ליען מלאכים צוווייי.

און ער הויבט ...
און בענטשט ד...

*Halb tunkl iz in tsimer, a roykhik lempl brent,*
*tsen orkhim-shotns vign zikh oyf vent.*

*Nor in tunkelstn vinkl a likhtik kinder-rod*
*un di mame dertseylt fun got's genod:*

*". . . Iz der betler gegangen a tog mit a nakht.*
*Gekumen tsum palats, der toyer farmakht.*

*Hot der betler gegebn dos ringl a drey,*
*zenen gekumen tsu flien malokhim tsvey*

**22**

dark in the room, a smoky lamp is burning,
...anger shadows on the walls are turning.

But in the darkest corner a radiant children-ring
and the mother telling of God's blessing:

". . . So the beggar walked for a day and night,
came to the palace, the portals shut tight.

So the beggar gave his ring a spin.
There came flying two seraphim.

ב געעפֿנט די זילבערנע טיר  
ער — די גאָלדענע טיר.

ללער געלאַכט און פֿאַריאָגט די נויט  
ין צו זעט אי וויין, אי ברויט..."

אם צימער. דער טיש איז געגרייט,  
רומען: „שוין שפּעט! שוין שפּעט!"

ר צענטער מיט אַ לויטער געזיכט  
אָפּ בליצט אויף אַ ליכט.

אויף די הענט און בענטשט די נויט  
לעגענדע פֿון וויין און ברויט.

---

*Hot eyner gëefnt di zilberne tir*
*un der tsveyter — di goldene tir.*

*Hot der betler gelakht un faryogt di noyt*
*un gehat shoyn tsu zat i vayn, i broyt. . . "*

*Halb tunkl dos tsimer. Der tish iz gegreyt,*
*nayn orkhim brumen: "Shoyn shpet! Shoyn shpet!"*

*Nor s'shteyt der tsenter mit a loyter gezikht*
*un iber zayn kop blitst oyf a likht.*

*Un er hoybt oyf di hent un bentsht di noyt*
*un bentsht di legende fun vayn un broyt.*

**22**

One of them opened the silver door,
and the second opened the golden door.

So the beggar laughed and poverty fled
and he had enough wine, enough bread. . . "

Half-dark in the room. The table waits.
Nine strangers grumble, "It's late! It's late!"

But the tenth one stands and lucidly gazes
and over his head a light blazes.

And he raises his hands and blesses the need
and blesses the legend of wine and bread.

# קין און חבל

„הבל, מיין ברודער, דו שלאָפסט
און דו ביזט אזוי וואונדערלערך שיין,
אזוי שיין ווי דו ביזט אצינד
האָב איך דיך נאָך נישט געזען..."

„ליגט די שיינקייט אין מיין האַק,
צי אפשר גאָר אין דיר?
איידער דער טאָג פארגייט,
זאָג, ענטפער מיר!" —

„הבל, ברודער, דו שוויינגסט,
ווי דער הימל און די ערד,
אזוי שוויינגן טיף און פארקלערט
האָב איך דיך נאָך נישט געהערט."

## KEYN UN HEVL

*Hevl, mayn bruder, du shlofst*
*un du bist azoy vunderlekh sheyn,*
*azoy sheyn vi du bizt atsind*
*hob ikh dikh nokh nisht gezen. . .*

*Ligt di sheynkayt in mayn hak,*
*tsi efsher gor in dir?*
*Eyder der tog fargeyt,*
*zog, entfer mir! —*

*Hevl, bruder, du shvaygst,*
*vi der himl un di erd,*
*azoy shvaygn tif un farklert*
*hob ikh dikh nokh nisht gehert.*

# 23

# ITZIK MANGER

## CAIN AND ABEL

Abel, my brother, you sleep
and you are wonderfully comely;
as fair as you now are
I have never seen you be.

    Does the beauty lie in my axe,
    or does it lie in you?
    Before the day has gone,
    speak to me. Reply!

Abel, my brother, you are mute
as the sky and earth;
such deep and musing silence
I have never heard.

„ליגט דאָס שוויײגן אין מיין האַק,
צי אפֿשר גאָר אין דיר?
אײדער דער טאָג פֿאַרגײט,
זאָג, ענטפֿער מיר!" —


„אָט שטײ איך נעבן דיר
און דו ביסט אזױ אַלײן,
אזױ פֿרעמד און אָפּגעשײדט
האָב איך דיך נאָך נישט געזען."


„ליגט די פֿרעמדקײט אין מיין האַק,
צי אַפֿשר גאָר אין דיר?
אײדער דער טאָג פֿאַרגײט,
זאָג, ענטפֿער מיר!"


*Ligt dos shvaygn in mayn hak,*
*tsi efsher gor in dir?*
*Eyder der tog fargeyt,*
*zog, entfer mir!* —

*Ot shtey ikh nebn dir*
*un du bizt azoy aleyn,*
*azoy fremd un opgesheydt*
*hob ikh dikh nokh nisht gezen.*

*Ligt di fremdkayt in mayn hak,*
*tsi efsher gor in dir?*
*Eyder der tog fargeyt,*
*zog, entfer mir!* —

**23**

Does the silence lie in my axe,
or does it lie in you?
Before the day has gone,
speak to me. Reply!

Here I stand beside you,
yet you are so lonely;
to find you alien and apart
I never thought to see.

Does the strangeness lie in my axe,
or does it lie in you?
Before the day has gone,
speak to me. Reply!

„קום, מוטער חוה, און זע,
ווי מיין ברודער הבל ליגט,
אזוי שא און שטיל און פֿאַרטראַכט
האָסטו אים נאָך נישט פֿאַרווינגט".


„ליגט די שטילקייט אין מיין האַק,
צי אפֿשר גאָר אין דיר?
אײדער דער טאָג פֿאַרגײט,
זאָג, ענטפֿער מיר!" —


„קום, פֿאָטער אדם, און זע
דאָס רויטע שנירל בלוט,
וואָס שלענגלט זיך אויף דער ערד
און שמעקט אזוי טרויעריק און גוט".


„ליגט דער טרויער אין מיין האַק,
צי אפֿשר גאָר אין דיר?
אײדער דער טאָג פֿאַרגײט,
זאָג, ענטפֿער מיר!" —


Kum, muter Khave, un ze,
vi mayn bruder Hevl ligt,
azoy sha un shtil un fartrakht
hostu im nokh nisht farvigt.

Ligt di shtilkayt in mayn hak,
tsi efsher gor in dir?
Eyder der tog fargeyt,
zog, entfer mir! —

Kum, foter Odem, un ze
dos royte shnirl blut,
vos shlenglt zikh oyf der erd
un shmekt azoy troyerik un gut.

Ligt der troyer in mayn hak,
tsi efsher gor in dir?
Eyder der tog fargeyt,
zog, entfer mir! —

**23**

Come, Mother Eve, and see
how my brother Abel lies;
more calm and still and rapt
than from your lullabies.

    Does the calm lie in my axe,
    or does it lie in you?
    Before the day has gone,
    speak to me. Reply!

Come, Father Adam, and see
the red thread of blood
that snakes along the ground
and smells so sorrowful and good.

    Does the sorrow lie in my axe,
    or does it lie in you?
    Before the day is gone,
    speak to me. Reply!

הגרס לעצטע נאַכט בײַ אַבֿרהמען

די שיפחה הגר זיצט אין קיך,
אַ רויכיק לעמפּל ברענט
און שאָטנס סאַמע קעץ און מײַז
אויף אַלע גראָע װענט.

זי װיינט. סע האָט דער באַלעבאָס
איר הײַנט געהייסן גיין.
„קליפּה", האָט ער איר געזאָגט,
„דו טרעטסט מיך אָפּ, צי ניין?"

סורציע די פּושקע-גאַבעטע
האָט אים שוין װידער אָנגערעדט:
„אָדער דו טרײַבסט די דינסט אַרױס,
אַז נישט װיל איך אַ גט".

# HOGORS LETSTE NAKHT BAY AVROMEN

*Di shifkhe Hogor zist in kikh,*
*a roykhik lempl brent*
*un shotns same kets un mayz*
*oyf ale groe vent.*

*Zi veynt. Se hot der balebos*
*ir haynt geheysn geyn.*
*"Klipe," hot er ir gezogt,*
*"du tretst mikh op, tsi neyn?"*

*Surtsye di pushke-gabete*
*hot im shoyn vider ongeredt:*
*"Oder du traybst di dinst aroys,*
*az nisht vil ikh a get."*

# 24

## ITZIK MANGER

### HAGAR'S LAST NIGHT AT ABRAHAM'S

In the kitchen the servant Hagar sits,
smoky lamplight falls
and shadows, very cats and mice,
on all the grey walls.

She cries. Today the master
has bidden her go.
"Leech," he said to her,
"Will you leave me, or no?"

Sarah the pious plunderer
has threatened him perforce:
"Either you drive that servant out
or give me a divorce."

און הגר נעמט פֿון קופֿערט אַרויס
אַ בײַטשל קרעלן װי בלוט,
אַ פֿאַרטעכל פֿון גרינעם זײַד
און אַ שטרױענעם זומערהוט.

די זאַכן האָט ער איר געשענקט,
אַ מאָל װען זיי זענען געגאַן
שפּאַצירן איבער דער לאָנקע,
דאָרט, װאו עס גייט די באַן.

„אױ, אַזױ װי אַ רױך פֿון אַ קױמען
און אַזױ װי אַ רױך פֿון אַ באַן,
אַזױ איז, מאַמע געטרײַע,
די ליבע פֿון אַ מאַן.

Un Hogor nemt fun kufert aroys
a baytshl kreln vi blut,
a fartekhl fun grinem zayd
un a shtroyenem zumerhut.

Di zakhn hot er ir geshenkt,
a mol ven zey zenen gegan
shpatsirn iber der lonke
dort, vu es geyt di ban.

"Oy, azoy vi a roykh fun a koymen
un azoy vi a roykh fun a ban,
azoy iz, mame getraye,
di libe fun a man.

And from the coffer Hagar takes
a string of beads like blood,
an apron of green silk
and a summer hat of straw.

He gave her these things,
when they were once
strolling through the meadow,
there, where the train runs.

"O, like the smoke of a chimney
and like the smoke of a train,
so, faithful mother,
is the love of a man.

וואו וועל איך מיך איצט אהינטון
מיטן פיצל קינד אויף די הענט?
סיידן נעמען זיין בענקאַרט
און גיין דינען אין דער פרעמד".

זי נעמט אין דער האַנט דעם בעזעם
און קערט צום לעצטן מאָל די שטוב
און עפעס אונטער דער בלוזקע
פילט, אז ס'האָט אים נאָך ליב.

זי וואַשט נאָך איין מאָל די טעלער
און שייערט די קופּערנע פֿאַן —
אזוי ווי אַ רויך פֿון אַ קוימען
איז די ליבע פֿון אַ מאַן.

*Vu vel ikh mikh itst ahintun*
*mitn pitsl kind oyf di hent?*
*Saydn nemen zayn benkart*
*un geyn dinen in der fremd."*

*Zi nemt in der hant dem bezem*
*un kert tsum letstn mol di shtub*
*un epes unter der bluzke*
*filt, az s'hot im nokh lib.*

*Zi vasht nokh eyn mol di teler*
*un shayert di kuperne fan —*
*azoy vi a roykh fun a koymen*
*iz di libe fun a man.*

**24**

"What will I do with myself
with the little one on my hands?
Unless I take his bastard
and serve in foreign lands."

She picks up the broom
and sweeps for the last time,
and something under her blouse
feels that she still loves him.

She washes the dishes just once more
and scours the copper pan —
like the smoke of a chimney
is the love of a man.

עקדת יצחק

— וואָס זעסטו איצטער, מיין קינד און קרבן?
— איך זע: איבערן ליכטיקן הימל־בלאָ
ציט אויס די פליגל אַ שווערע טיפע שעה
און אויף אַ צלם העענגט אַ מענטש געשטאָרבן.

וואָס שטייסטו, פֿאָטער, אַזוי בלייך און שטום,
און ס׳גליטשט דיין מעסער זיך אַראָפ צו דר׳ערד?
— דיין שיינער טויט איז אַן אַנדערן באַשערט,
טו אָן דיין טרויער, מיין קינד, און קום.

*EKEYDES YITSKHOK*

*— Vos zestu itster, mayn kind un korbn?*
*— Ikh ze: ibern likhtikn himl-blo*
*tsit oys di fligl a shvere tife sho*
*un oyf a tseylem hengt a mentsh geshtorbn.*

*Vos shteystu, foter, azoy bleykh un shtum,*
*un s'glitsht dayn meser zikh arop tsu dr'erd?*
*— Dayn sheyner toyt iz an andern bashert,*
*tu on dayn troyer, mayn kind, un kum.*

**25**

# ITZIK MANGER

## THE BINDING OF ISAAC

— What do you see now, my child and offering?
— I see: in the glowing sky-blue overhead
a heavy, deep hour's wings are spread
and on a cross a dead man hangs.

Why do you stand, Father, so pale and dumb,
and your knife slips downward to the ground?
— Your lovely death to another's fate is bound.
Put on your sorrow, my child, and come.

— װער איז ער, װער? איך װיל זײן פנים זען.
הײליק דאַרף ער זײן און אױסטערליש און שײן —
אָט דער, װאָס האָט מײן קרבן צוגענומען!

— קום, קינד, דער אָװנט טונקלט שױן אין פעלד.
דער װעג איז לאַנג און װײט נאָך דאָס געצעלט,
און ער, דער גליקלעכער, ער דאַרף ערשט קומען.

— Ver iz er, ver? Ikh vil zayn ponem zen.
Heylik darf er zayn un oysterlish un sheyn —
ot der, vos hot mayn korbn tsugenumen!

— Kum, kind, der ovnt tunklt shoyn in feld.
Der veg iz lang un vayt nokh dos getselt,
un er, der gliklekher, er darf ersht kumen.

**25**

— Who is he, who? I want to see his face.
Holy he must be and rare and beautiful —
that one who took my sacrifice away!

— Come, child, on the field night descends.
Far and long is the journey to our tents,
and he, the happy one, has yet to come.

# אויפן שיידוועג

אויפן שיידוועג זינגט דער זומערווינט:
— די וועגן זענען אלט,
איין וועג צום דארף, איין וועג צו גאָט,
דער דריטער וועג צום וואַלד.

## OYFN SHEYDVEG

Oyfn sheydveg zingt der zumervint:
— Di vegn zenen alt,
eyn veg tsum dorf, eyn veg tsu got,
der driter veg tsum vald.

# 26

# ITZIK MANGER

## AT THE CROSSROAD
### (Naomi and her daughters-in-law)

At the crossroad the summer wind sings:
— The roads are old,
one road to the village, one road to God,
the third road to the wood.

דער וועג וואָס פירט צום ווילדן וואַלד,
דאָס איז דער וועג פון טויט.
דער וועג וואָס פירט צום שטילן דאָרף,
דאָס איז דער וועג פון ברויט.

דער דריטער וועג וואָס פירט צו גאָט
דאָס איז דער וועג פון פרייד,
ווייל גאָט איז פרייד און איבער-פרייד,
גאָט איז אייביקייט.

נעמי האָרכט. איר האַרץ פאַרשטייט
וואָס ס׳זינגט דער זומערווינט,
זי האָט זיין פּלאַפּל שוין געהערט
אין וויגל נאָך, אַ קינד.

*Der veg vos firt tsum vildn vald,*
*dos iz der veg fun toyt.*
*Der veg vos firt tsum shtiln dorf,*
*dos iz der veg fun broyt.*

*Der driter veg vos firt tsu got*
*dos iz der veg fun freyd,*
*vayl got is freyd un iber-freyd,*
*got iz eybikayt.*

*Nomi horkht. Ir harts farshteyt*
*vos s'zingt der zumervint,*
*zi hot zayn plapl shoyn gehert*
*in vigl nokh, a kind.*

The road that leads to the wild wood
is the road of the dead.
The road that leads to the quiet village,
that is the road of bread.

The third road leads to God,
is the way of felicity,
for God is joy and above joy,
God is eternity.

Naomi listens. Her heart knows
what the summer wind sings.
She had heard his babble
in her crib, as a nursling.

זי אָטעמט טיף. סע'שמעקט אין פעלד
מיט פריש-געשניטן היי,
פאַר וואָס זשע טוט דאָס שיידן איר
אַזש ביז צו טרערן וויי?

און נעמי זאָגט: „הערט, טעכטער, הערט,
וואָס ס'האָט צו זיין זאָל זיין,
מיר פראַווען די לעצטע סעודה דאָ
מיט קאָרנברויט און וויין."

זיי זעצן זיך ביים ראַנד פון וועג
און פראַווען די סעודה שטיל,
פון דער ווייטנס ווינקט צו זיי
די אַלטע פאַרלאָזטע מיל.

*Zi otemt tif. Se shmekt in feld*
*mit frish-geshnitn hey,*
*far vos zhe tut dos sheydn ir*
*azh biz tsu trern vey?*

*Un Nomi zogt: "Hert, tekhter, hert,*
*vos s'hot tsu zayn zol zayn,*
*mir praven di letste sude do*
*mit kornbroyt un vayn."*

*Zey zetsn zikh baym rand fun veg*
*un praven di sude shtil,*
*fun der vaytns vinkt tsu zey*
*di alte farlozte mil.*

**26**

The field smells of fresh-mown hay.
She breathes deep.
Why does the parting hurt her so
that she must weep?

"Hear daughters, hear, what must be,
must be," Naomi said.
"We celebrate our last supper here
with wine and corn bread."

They sit down at the roadside
and eat the supper tranquilly.
From afar the old deserted mill
blinks at the three.

די אַלטע גוטע פֿאַרלאָזטע מיל
שטרעקט אויס די הענט צו זיי:
— איך האָב אייך יאָרן געטריי געדינט,
פֿאָר וואָס טוט איר מיר וויי?

די ליפּעבביימער פּאַזע וועג,
זיי זענען מיד און אַלט.
זיי רוישן היינט ווי אַלע מאָל
די בענקשאַפֿט צו דעם וואַלד.

די פֿרויען זיצן פּאַזע וועג
און פּראַווען די סעודה שטום
און איבער די דריי אַלמנה-קעפּ
פֿלאַטערן שוואַלבן פֿרום.

*Di alte gute farlozte mil*
*shtrekt oys di hent tsu zey:*
*— Ikh hob aykh yorn getray gedint,*
*far vos tut ir mir vey?*

*Di lipebeymer paze veg,*
*zey zenen mid un alt.*
*Zey royshn haynt vi ale mol*
*di benkshaft tsu dem vald.*

*Di froyen zitsn paze veg*
*un praven di sude shtum*
*un iber di dray almone-kep*
*flatern shvalbn frum.*

The old kind deserted mill
stretches out its hands to the three:
— Why do you hurt me so? For years
I served you loyally.

The roadside linden trees
are aging and depressed.
As always, today they rustle
their longing for the forest.

The women sit at the roadside
and mutely celebrate the meal.
And over the three widow-heads
pious swallows wheel.

# אָוונט גאַנג

טראָט ביי טראָט, טראָט ביי טראָט,
יעדער טראָט אַן עשאַפאָט.
טיגער־אויגן, גרינע שטערן
און די שטילקייט וויינט אַן טרערן.

גיי איך מיט מיין דאָרן־קראַנץ
אין דעם רויטן אָוונט־גלאַנץ,
ווי אַ קלייד אין בלוט געטרונקען
איז אויף מיר דער טוי געזונקען.

*OVNT GANG*

*Trot bay trot, trot bay trot,*
*yeder trot an eshafot.*
*Tiger-oygn, grine shtern*
*un di shtilkayt veynt on trern.*

*Gey ikh mit mayn dorn-krants*
*in dem roytn ovnt-glants,*
*vi a kleyd in blut getrunken*
*iz oyf mir der toy gezunken.*

# 27

## DAVID EINHORN

### EVENING WALK

Step by step, step by step,
every step a scaffold.
Green stars, tiger eyes,
tearlessly the silence cries.

In my thorn crown I go
through the red evening glow,
like a gown dyed in blood's hue
I was drenched by the dew.

אזוי גיי איך אונטערטעניק
אינעם פּורפּור פֿון אַ קיניג
מיט מיין טויזנט־יאַריקער לאַסט
צו דעם שוואַרצן נאַכט פּאַלאַסט.

ווי די גרויע קראַען שרייען!
באַלד וועט מיך די נאַכט באַפֿרייען
און מיט קאַלטן וואַלד־גערויש
מיך פֿאַרוויגן אין איר שויס.

*Azoy gey ikh untertenik*
*inem purpur fun a kinig*
*mit mayn toyznt-yoriker last*
*tsu dem shvartsn nakht palast.*

*Vi di groye kroen shrayen!*
*Bald vet mikh di nakht bafrayen*
*un mit kaltn vald-geroysh*
*mikh farvign in ir shoys.*

So I walk in humbleness
in a monarch's purple dress
with my thousand-year-old weight
to the palace of the night.

How the grey ravens croak!
The night shall soon take off my yoke
and with the rustle of the cold forest
in her lap rock me to rest.

# דער אָנזאָגער

דער אָנזאָגער קומט פֿאַרטאָג
אָן אָפּגעשליסענער,
פֿון הינט אַ צעביסענער.
דער אָנזאָגער איז שטום.
ער וואַשט ביים קוואַל די וואונדן,
וואָס ער האָט גיך פֿאַרבונדן
און קוקט זיך אַרום.
זײַן שליחות איז פֿרייד,
אין די טרויעריקסטע פֿאַרטאָגן
אָן רייד אָנצוזאָגן.

---

## DER ONZOGER

*Der onzoger kumt fartog*
*an opgeshlisener,*
*fun hint a tsebisener.*
*Der onzoger iz shtum.*
*Er vasht baym kval di vundn,*
*vos er hot gikh farbundn*
*un kukt zikh arum.*
*Zayn shlikhes iz freyd,*
*in di troyerikste fartogn*
*on reyd ontsuzogn.*

# 28

## J. GLATSTEIN

## THE MESSENGER

The messenger comes at dawn
all in rags,
bitten by dogs.
The messenger is mute.
He washes his wounds at the spring,
quickly bandaging,
and looks about.
His message is joy,
in dawns of dreariness
silently professed.

די גאַס איז טויט, אַ משוגענע מויד,
זיצט אויף אַ פאַס
און ווערט צעזעצט פון געלעכטער.
ס׳דרימלט אַן אַלטער, טויבער וועכטער
ביי אַ צעפלינדערט הויז.
דער אָנזאַגער קען אים נישט דערוועקן.
די משוגענע מויד עפנט ס׳מויל און שעלט.
דער אָנזאַגער לויפט,
אָבער ס׳יאָגן אים נאָך די שרעקן
פון אַ טויטער וועלט.

Di gas iz toyt, a meshugene moyd,
zitst oyf a fas
un vert tsezetst fun gelekhter.
S'drimlt an alter, toyber vekhter
bay a tseplindert hoyz.
Der onzoger ken im nisht dervekn.
Di meshugene moyd efnt s'moyl un shelt.
Der onzoger loyft,
ober s'yogn im nokh di shrekn
fun a toyter velt.

**28**

The street is dead, a crazy girl
sits on a cask
and splits, laughing, at the seams.
An old deaf watchman dreams
before a plundered house.
The messenger cannot arouse him.
The crazy girl opens her mouth to curse.
The messenger flees
but he is pursued by the horrors
of a dead universe.

# CHILDREN STILL DIE OF FEAR

This group of poems could have been and perhaps should have been much larger. Hunger, pogrom, Nazi slaughter, medieval Inquisition, anti-Semitism, village and city misery, are the subjects of the overwhelming number of Yiddish poems. Here are some of the representative types: Landau's low keyed notation, Melech Ravitch's more direct and subjective accusation. The anti-war poem is seen in J. Adler's timeless litany, and the perpetual feeling of guilt for being free from catastrophe is expressed in Auerbach's "Grey Uncles." Glatstein measures three angles of the problem, and in three different ways. Of these, his "Ghetto Song," a bittersweet lullaby, is surely one of the best World War II poems in any language. A. Almi's "Everywhere" takes for granted, in the forced wisdom of recognizing the inevitable, the universal quality (quantity, one might say) of suffering. His almost shrug of the shoulders is an articulation of one way to manage to live until tomorrow.

# שטיל לאָמיר אַלע פאַרשווינדן

שטיל לאָמיר אַלע פאַרשווינדן,
קום נאָר דער אָוונט דערוואַכט,
גאָלדיק די שטערן זיך צינדן,
פאָרן אַוועק מיט דער נאַכט.

לאָמיר זיין גלייך צו די שטערן,
שווימען מיר אַלע אַוועק.
שטיל, עס זאָל קיינער ניט הערן —
שטאַרבן דאָך קינדער פון שרעק.

# SHTIL LOMIR ALE FARSHVINDN

Shtil lomir ale farshvindn,
koym nor der ovnt dervakht,
goldik di shtern zikh tsindn,
forn avek mit der nakht.

Lomir zayn glaykh tsu di shtern,
shvimen mir ale avek.
Shtil, es zol keyner nit hern —
shtarbn dokh kinder fun shrek.

# 29

## ZISHA LANDAU

### SOFTLY LET US ALL VANISH

Softly let us all vanish
just as the evening awakes;
stars grow golden with light,
riding away with the night.

Let us be like the stars,
then we will all swim away.
Softly, lest anyone hear —
children still die of fear.

# היינט האבן די נאצי-חילות . . .

היינט האבן די נאצי-חילות דורך מיין שטעטל אין פוילן
אדורכמארשירט.
און איך בין פון וייטן און וואויל איז צו מיר —
אומשטיינס מיר געזאגט,
באהאלטן זיך אויף דעם זיכערסטן פלאץ
אויף דער ערד
און א לידל שרייב איך נאך אויך, איך פאיאץ,
און גראמען צום בלוטיקן לידל
האב איך מיר צוגעקלערט,
עס פעלט נאר צום רומל — עס זאל זיין א סאנעט —
און פארוואס טאקע נישט?

*HAYNT HOBN DI NATSI-KHAYULES . . .*

*Haynt hobn di natsi-khayules durkh mayn shtetl in poyln*
    *adurkhmarshirt.*
*Un ikh bin fun vaytn un voyl iz tsu mir —*
*umshteyns mir gezogt,*
*bahaltn zikh oyf dem zikherstn plats*
*oyf der erd*
*un a lidl shrayb ikh nokh oykh, ikh payats,*
*un gramen tsum blutikn lidl*
*hob ikh mir tsugeklert,*
*es felt nor tsum ruml — es zol zayn a sonet —*
*un farvos take nisht?*

# 30

## MELECH RAVITCH

## TODAY THE NAZI FORCES MARCHED

Today the Nazi forces marched through my village in
    Poland.
And I am far away and happy am I —
some happiness!
Have hidden myself in the safest place
in the world
and I even write a song, I — jester.
I have invented
rhymes for the blood-stained song —
only some lines are missing to make it a sonnet —
and why not?

כבין היינט אויפגעשטאַנען פון אַ קלאָרן בעט,
און געגעסן ברויט און געטרונקען מילך.
און — מיין מאַמע איז אין קעלער געלעגן אין אונדזער אַלטן הויז,
און אַ סקאָרינקע געגריזשעט אַזוי ווי אַ מויז.

אַז ווי איז צו מיר — כהאָב דאָך היינט שפּאַצירט אין אַ פרייער גאַס,
וואָלקנס אין הימל געזען, וואָלקנס באַגילדט פון דער זון,
און פריינט געטראָפן און געמאַכט מיט זיי שפּאַס.
און — היינט נאַכט וועט מיין מאַמע קריכן פון קעלער אויף אַלע פיר
אָטעם צו כאַפּן, צו טאָן אויף דער נאַכטיקער וועלט אַ בליק,
און פּלוצלונג וועט זיך אַ שאָרך דערהערן,
וועט זי אין קעלער אַריין צוריק
אַנטלויפן און זיך האַלטן האַרט ביי דער מויער,
און אויף אַלע פיר — ווי אַ שפּייכלער־טכויער.


*Kh'bin haynt oyfgeshtanen fun a klorn bet,*
*un gegesn broyt un getrunken milkh.*
*Un — mayn mame iz in keler gelegn in undzer altn hoyz,*
*un a skorinke gegrizhet azoy vi a moyz.*

*Az vey iz tsu mir — kh'hob dokh haynt shpatsirt in a*
    *frayer gas,*
*volkns in himl gezen, volkns bagildt fun der zun,*
*un fraynt getrofn un gemakht mit zey shpas.*
*Un — haynt nakht vet mayn mame krikhn fun keler oyf*
    *ale fir*
*otem tsu khapn, tsu ton oyf der nakhtiker velt a blik,*
*un plutslung vet zikh a shorkh derhern,*
*vet zi in keler arayn tsurik*
*antloyfn un zikh haltn hart bay der moyer,*
*un oyf ale fir — vi a shpaykhler-tkhoyer.*

**30**

Today I rose from a clean bed,
and ate bread and drank milk.
And — my mother lay in the cellar of our old house,
gnawed at a crust of bread like a mouse.

Woe is me — today I strolled on a free street,
saw clouds in the sky, clouds gilded with sun,
and met with friends and had some fun.
And — tonight my mother will crawl on all fours from the
    cellar
to get some air, to take a look at the night-time world;
suddenly she will hear a rustle,
and escaping back into the cellar
she will run and close to the wall she will squat
on all fours — like a granary cat.

אַז וויי איז צו מיר, כ׳האָב היינט דאָך מיט מענטשן זיך
פריינטלעך געגריסט,
גערעדט וועגן קריג, וועגן דייטש און פראַנצויז,
און — מיין מאַמע האָט אַ גאַנצן טאָג געשוויגן
אין קעלער אין אונדזער אַלטן הויז,
אויף אַ סטויגעלע האָלץ געלעגן, און האָט זיך איינגעהערט
ווי עס ציטערט דאָס הויז איבער איר, אונטער איר — די ערד.
איר טייער האַרץ האָט כּסדר געקלאַפּט, ווי מיט לעצטע קלעפּ.
ווי מען האַקט אין ווענט מיט מענטשלעכע קעפּ,
ווי מיט לעצטע טראָפּנס — רינט אַ וואונד.

ווי אַ קיילעכל געלעגן איינגעניורעט אין זיך,
ווי אַן אָפּגעשטראָפטער — אַ דערשלאָגענער הונט
פון אַ מערדער — אַ באַלעבאָס,
און ווי דער הונט נישט געוואוסט פאַרוואָס.

*Az vey iz tsu mir, kh'hob haynt dokh mit mentshn zikh*
    *frayntlekh gegrist,*
*geredt vegn krig, vegn daytsh un frantsoyz,*
*un — mayn mame hot a gantsn tog geshvign*
*in keler in undzer altn hoyz,*
*oyf a stoygele holts gelegn, un hot zikh ayngehert*
*vi es tsitert dos hoyz iber ir, unter ir — di erd.*
*Ir tayer harts hot keseyder keklapt, vi mit letste klep.*
*Vi men hakt in vent mit mentshlekhe kep,*
*vi mit letste tropns — rint a vund.*

*Vi a kaylekhl gelegn ayngenyuret in zikh,*
*vi an opgeshtrofter — a dershlogener hunt*
*fun a merder — a balabos,*
*un vi der hunt nisht gevust farvos.*

Woe is me, today I exchanged greetings with friends,
talked of the war, of the Germans and French.
And — all day my mother spoke not one word
in the cellar of our old house;
she lay on a small pile of wood — ears alert
to the shudder of the house above her, under her —
    the earth.
Her dear heart kept pounding, as if each beat were the last,
like human heads knocked against walls,
like a wound bled of its final drops.

Like a ball, she lay curled up in herself,
like the punished, the dejected dog
of a murderous master,
and like that dog — did not understand.

און פלוצלונג איז אין אין ווינקל, אין דעם פולן קעלער,
אָנגעפּאַקט ווי צו כל נדרי אַ שול,
די מאַמע אַזוי ווי משוגע געוואָרן און האָט
אַ ווילדן געשריי געטאָן: מענטשן —
מיר דאַכט זיך, אַז ס'איז נישטאָ אויף דער וועלט קיין גאָט —

דער פולער קעלער האָט דעם אָטעם אינגאַנצן איינגעהאַלטן,
און האָט זיך נאָך טיפער באַהאַלטן,
און זיך נאָך שטאַרקער איינגעהערט,
ווי עס ציטערט פון אויבן דאָס הויז און פון אונטן — די ערד.

*Un plutslung iz in vinkl, in dem fuln keler,*
*ongepakt vi tsu kol nidre a shul,*
*di mame azoy vi meshuge gevorn un hot*
*a vildn geshrey geton: Mentshn —*
*mir dakht zikh, az s'iz nishto oyf der velt kayn got —*

*Der fuler keler hot dem otem ingantsn ayngehaltn,*
*un hot zikh nokh tifer bahaltn,*
*un zikh nokh shtarker ayngehert,*
*vi es tsitert fun oybn dos hoyz un fun untn — di erd.*

**30**

And suddenly in the corner of that full cellar,
packed like a synagogue for Kol Nidre,
my mother, as if crazed,
gave a wild shriek: People,
it seems to me that there is no God in this world —

The full cellar held its breath completely,
and hid itself more deeply,
and strained, even more alert,
to the shudder of the house above, and underneath -
    the earth.

Kol Nidre: literally "all vows," a prayer before Yom Kippur,
the most important holy day of the year.

# צייט-ליד

מיר וועלן קיין קאָרן, קיין וױיץ און קיין גערשטן
ניט האָבן —
די פעלדער, די ברײטע, זײ שטײען אין גריבער
צעגראָבן.

מיר וועלן קיין שאָף און קיין רינד אױפֿ'ן פֿעלד מער
ניט האָבן —
די פעלדער, זײ זײנען פֿערנומען מיט מתים
און ראָבן...

די בוימער, זײ שטײען באַלאָדן מיט עפּל
און באַרן —
זײ וועלן אַזױ אױף די צוױיגן פֿאַרפֿױלען,
פֿערדאַרען...

## TSAYT-LID

*Mir veln kayn korn, kayn veyts un kayn gershtn*
*nit hobn —*
*di felder, di breyte, zey shteyn in griber*
*tsegrobn.*

*Mir veln kayn shof un kayn rind oyfn feld mer*
*nit hobn —*
*di felder, zey zaynen farnumen mit meysim*
*un robn . . .*

*Di boymer, zey shteyn belodn mit epl*
*un barn —*
*zey veln azoy oyf di tsvaygn farfoyln,*
*fardarn . . .*

## J. ADLER

## SONG OF THE TIMES

No corn, no wheat, and no barley
shall be had —
the fields, the broad fields, in graves
are clad.

No more will sheep and oxen in our fields
find haven —
the fields, the fields are busied with corpse
and raven . . .

The trees, they stand burdened with apple
and pear —
and so will they rot, dry up, and the branches
grow bare . . .

די יונגסטע, די קרעפֿטיגסטע מענשען, זיי שטייען
אין פֿלאַקער —
ניטאָ ווער ס׳זאָל זייען און פֿלאַנצען און פֿירען
דעם אַקער.

די פֿעלדער, זיי זיינען פֿערנומען מיט מתים
און ראָבען —
מיר וועלן קיין קאָרן, קיין ווייץ און קיין גערשטען
ניט האָבן . . .

*Di yungste, di kreftikste mentshn, zey shteyn*
*in flaker —*
*nito ver s'zol zeyen un flantsn un firn*
*dem aker.*

*Di felder, zey zaynen farnumen mit meysim*
*un robn —*
*mir veln kayn korn, kayn veyts un kayn gershtn*
*nit hobn . . .*

**31**

The youngest, the mightiest men, are fighting
in fire now —
there is no one to sow and to plant and to guide
the plow.

The fields, the fields are busied with ravens
and the dead —
no corn, no wheat, and no barley
shall be had . . .

# דאָ בין איך קיינמאָל נישט געווען

כ'האָב אַלעמאָל געמיינט
איך בין שוין דאָ געוועזן.
מיט יעדן יאָר פֿון מיין איבערגעניצעוועט לעבן
האָב איך געוואַרעמט געוועבן
פֿון אָפּגעלעבטע שטיקער וועלט.
איך האָב דערקענט געדענקטע פּנים'ער און שמייכלען
און אַפֿילו טאַטע-מאַמע זײַנען פֿאַר מיר געווען
פֿאַרבענקטע פֿרעסקאָס אַמאָליקייט.
כ'האָב געטראָטן אויף אַלטע רשעות'דיקע שטעגן
און צווישן ברעגן פֿון געשיכטע
האָב איך געזעגלט.

## DO BIN IKH KEYNMOL NISHT GEVEN

*Kh'hob alemol gemeynt*
*ikh bin shoyn do gevezn.*
*Mit yeden yor fun mayn ibergenitsevet lebn*
*hob ikh gevaremt gevebn*
*fun opgelebte shtiker velt.*
*Ikh hob derkent gedenkte penemer un shmeykhlen*
*un afile tate-mame zaynen far mir geven*
*farbenkte freskos amolikayt.*
*Ikh hob getrotn oyf alte reshuesdike shtegn*
*un tsvishn bregn fun geshikhte*
*hob ikh gezeglt.*

# 32

## J. GLATSTEIN

### I HAVE NEVER BEEN HERE BEFORE

I had always thought
I had been here before.
With every year of my hand-me-down life
I had woven warmth
from worn-out pieces of the world.
I had noticed there remembered faces and smiles
and even father-mother had become for me
longing frescoes of once-upon-a-time.
I trod old paths of wickedness
and between the shores of history
I sailed.

איך האָב כסדר געפֿונען דאָס װאונדער,
װאָס איז אין געדעכעניש געװען איינגעקריצט,
און ס'האָט די אָפּגעטומעלטע פֿאַרגאַנגענהייט
זיך שעמעװדיק געבלעזלט אין דעם איצט.
איך האָב געמיינט
כ'בין שוין דאָ אַמאָל געװעזן.

נאָר די לעצטע שטיקלעך יאָרן־צױטן,
מיט די אױסגעטראַכטע טױטן,
זײַנען מײַנע אײגענע טעג און נעכט.
דאָס איז מײַן אָנגעהױקערטע באַשערטקײט,
דאָס האָב איך אַלײן זיך אָנגעלעבט.
די פֿאַרגליװערטע פֿאַרקלערטקײט,
פֿאַרברענטע פֿעלדער,
די מאַפּעס מיט בית־עלמין'ס,
פֿאַרשראָקענע שטילקײט,
די צײַכנס פֿון פֿרײדיקער רשעות —

*Ikh hob keseyder gefunen dos vunder,*
*vos iz in gedekhenish geven ayngekritst,*
*un s'hot di opgetumelte fargangenhayt*
*zikh shemevdik geblezlt in dem itst.*
*Ikh hob gemeynt*
*kh'bin shoyn do amol gevezn.*

*Nor di letste shtiklekh yorn-tsoytn,*
*mit di oysgetrakhte toytn,*
*zaynen mayne eygene teg un nekht.*
*Dos iz mayn ongehoykerte bashertkayt,*
*dos hob ikh aleyn zikh ongelebt.*
*Di fargliverte farklertkayt,*
*farbrente felder,*
*di mapes mit beys-almins,*
*farshrokene shtilkayt,*
*di tseykhns fun freydiker reshues —*

**32**

Time after time I found the wonder
that had been engraved in memory,
and the no longer noisy past
had modestly breathed itself into the now.
I thought
I had been here once before.

But these recent tag ends of years
with their fabricated deaths
*are* my own days and nights.
This is my hunchbacked destiny,
this I have alone achieved.
The congealed contemplation,
burned fields,
the maps of cemeteries,
terrified stillness,
the signs of joyous evil —

כ'האב עם פון ערגעץ נישט געדענקט.
כ'האב עם קיינמאל נישט געזען
כ'בין דא קיינמאל נישט געווען.

בלייב שטיל, טויטע וועלט.
שווייג איין אין זיך דיין פארוויסטקייט.
ס'וועלן ווידעראמאל בליען פארוויאנעטע ארנאמענטן.
מיר וועלן איבערבויען דיינע פונדאמענטן,
אויף דעם בלוט וואס מען האט פארגאסן.
נאר די טויטע וועלן וויינען אין די חצות'ן,
יעדער מת — א טריפנדיק קול.
ווי א קליין ליכטל איבער יעדן קבר,
וועט פלעמלען א געבעט.
יעדער פאר זיך.
איך בין איך —
וועלן טויזנטער געשאכטענע איכן
וויינען אין דער נאכט.

*kh'hob es fun ergets nisht gedenkt.*
*Kh'hob es keynmol nisht gezen,*
*kh'bin do keynmol nisht geven.*

*Blayb shtil, toyte velt.*
*Shvayg ayn in zikh dayn farvistkayt.*
*S'veln videramol bliyen farviante ornamentn.*
*Mir veln iberboyen dayne fundamentn,*
*oyf dem blut vos men hot fargosn.*
*Nor di toyte veln veynen in di khtsosn,*
*yeder mes — a trifndik kol.*
*Vi a kleyn likhtl iber yedn keyver,*
*vet flemlen a gebet.*
*Yeder far zikh.*
*Ikh bin ikh —*
*veln toyznter geshokhtene ikhn*
*veynen in der nakht.*

## 32

I remembered it from nowhere.
I had not ever seen it anywhere,
I have never been here before.

Be still, dead world.
Stifle within yourself your desolation.
Withered ornaments will bloom again.
We will rebuild your foundation
on the blood that has been shed.
At midnight there will weep only the dead;
each corpse will become a piercing shout.
Like a small light over every grave
a prayer will flicker.
Each for himself.
I am I —
Thousands of slaughtered I's
will weep in the night.

טויט בין איך און נישט דערקאַנט,
מײַן בלוט נאָך אַלץ נישט אויפֿגעמאַנט.

אַזאַ עשירות פֿון מצבֿות
האָב איך קײַנמאָל נישט געזען.
טאָג און נאַכט וועל איך יאָמערן די נעמען.

דאָ בין איך קײַנמאָל נישט געווען.

*Toyt bin ikh un nisht derkont,*
*mayn blut nokh alts nisht oyfgemont.*

*Aza ashires fun metseyves*
*hob ikh keynmol nisht gezen.*
*Tog un nakht vel ikh yomern di nemen.*

*Do bin ikh keynmol nisht geven.*

**32**

Dead am I and unknown,
my blood not yet accounted for.

Such a wealth of gravestones
I have never seen before.
Day and night I will lament the names.

I have never been here before.

# געטאָ-ליד

מיין געזאַנג אין דיינע ביינדלעך,
ווי יונגער שניי צעגייט.
אין דיינע שטערנדיקע אויגן,
וואַכט אויף אַן אַלטער פרייד.
לאַכעלע, מיין קינד,
זינגעניו, מיין טרויער,
ס'גייען אויף זיבן זונען
אויף אַן אַלטן מויער.

## GETO-LID

*Mayn gezang in dayne beyndlekh*
*vi yunger shney tsegeyt.*
*In dayne shterndike oygn*
*vakht oyf an alter freyd.*
*Lakhele, mayn kind,*
*zingenyu, mayn troyer,*
*s'geyen oyf zibn zunen*
*oyf an altn moyer.*

# 33

## J. GLATSTEIN

## GHETTO SONG

My song in your little bones
melts like early snows.
In your starlike eyes
an old delight grows.
Laugh a bit, my child,
sing, my agonizing.
On an ancient wall
seven suns are rising.

דער שבת ווינט א פֿאַרשוועכטער,
פֿון די בוימער־שפּיצן.
אויף אַלע חושכ׳דיקע געסלער
טויטע בעטלער זיצן.
שוויײגעניו, מײן קינד,
שלאָפֿעלע, מײן קרישל,
אויף דײַן ליידיקן טעלער,
טאַנצט אַ גילדן פֿישל.

שטערן פֿון אונטערוועגנס,
באַלײַכט דײַן טאַטנס וועג.
די לבֿנה איז זײַן פֿאַרמעגנס,
אויפֿן נאַכטיקן געיעג.
שלאָפֿעשי, מײן קינד,
קושעניו דײַנע אויגן,
איבער קלאָגנדיקע חורבֿות
איז אַ טײבעלע געפֿלויגן.

*Der shabes vint a farshvekhter,*
*fun di boymer-shpitsn.*
*Oyf ale khoyshekhdike geslekh*
*toyte betler zitsn.*
*Shvaygenyu, mayn kind,*
*shlofele, mayn krishl,*
*oyf dayn leydikn teler,*
*tantst a gildn fishl.*

*Shtern fun untervegns,*
*balaykht dayn tatns veg.*
*Di levone iz zayn farmegns,*
*oyfn nakhtikn geyeg.*
*Shlofeshi, mayn kind,*
*kushenyu dayne oygn,*
*iber klogndike khurves*
*iz a taybele gefloygn.*

The Sabbath wind desecrated
by the tree-top tips.
In all the darkened alleys
dead beggars sit.
Silently, my child,
sleep a bit, my midge.
A golden fish dances
in your empty dish.

Stars along the path
light your father's pace.
The moon is all he has
on the nightly chase.
Sleep a bit, my child,
I gently kiss your eyes.
Over wailing ruins
a little dove flies.

דאָס טײבעלע ביסטו דאָך,
דײנע הענטלעך װײסע פֿליגל.
דײן מאַמע װעט נישט אָפּטרעטן
פֿון דײן הונגעריק װיגל.
שאַזשעשי, מײן קינד,
שטילעניו, מײן טרױער.
דײן טאַטנס גוטע הענט
עפֿענען דעם טױער.

*Dos taybele bistu dokh,*
*dayne hentlekh vayse fligl.*
*Dayn mame vet nisht optretn*
*fun dayn hungerik vigl.*
*Shazheshi, mayn kind,*
*shtilenyu, mayn troyer.*
*Dayn tatns gute hent*
*efenen dem toyer.*

**33**

The little dove is you,
your hands wings of white.
Your mother will not leave
your hungry crib at night.
Hush, then, hush, my child,
be still a bit, my fate.
The good hands of your father
are opening the gate.

# גרויע פּעטערס

אַלע מיינע פּעטערס האָבן אָנגעטאָן זיך גרויע בערד,
האָבן זיך די פּנים'ער צעקנייטשט ווי אַלטע פֿעל
און זיך אויסגעשטעלט צום ווייטן וועג געקערט
ביי מיין חרוב'ער היים, אויף מיין חרוב'ער שוועל.

אַז זיי האָבן מיך דערזען פֿון ווייטנס, האָבן זיי געוויינט,
אויפֿן קול געוויינט:  מיר זענען וויסט און גרוי.
אָבער איך האָב נישט געגלייבט זיי און געמיינט,
אַז זיי האָבן זיך פֿאַר מיר פֿאַרשטעלט אַזוי.

האָב איך זיך צעלאַכט אויף דעם געוויין און זיי געזאָגט:
טוט זיך אויס די בערד און זייט מיר ווי אַמאָל,
זענען זיי געפֿאַלן אויף דער ערד און אויסגעקלאָגט
ס'ביטערקייט פֿון הערצער אויפֿן הויכן קול.

## GROYE FETERS

*Ale mayne feters hobn ongeton zikh groye berd,*
*hobn zikh di penemer tsekneytsht vi alte fel*
*un zikh oysgeshtelt tsum vaytn veg gekert*
*bay mayn khorever heym, oyf mayn khorever shvel.*

*Az zey hobn mikh derzen fun vaytns, hobn zey geveynt,*
*oyfn kol geveynt: mir zenen vist un groy.*
*Ober ikh hob nisht gegleybt zey un gemeynt,*
*az zey hobn zikh far mir farshtelt azoy.*

*Hob ikh zikh tselakht oyf dem geveyn un zey gezogt:*
*Tut zikh oys di berd un zayt mir vi amol.*
*Zenen zey gefaln oyf der erd un oysgeklogt*
*s'biterkayt fun hertser oyfn hoykhn kol.*

# EPHRAIM AUERBACH

## GREY UNCLES

All my uncles put on beards of grey.
Their faces going wrinkled like old hide,
they ranged themselves, facing the farthest way,
at my ruined house, at my bleak doorside.

When they saw me from afar they wept,
wept loudly: We are sere and grey.
But I did not believe them and I thought
they had disguised themselves in this array.

I laughed at their wailing and said:
Take off your beards and be as you used to be.
They fell to the earth and eased
their heart's bitterness by weeping noisily.

האָב איך אויסגעטאַפּט די בערד: גרוי און בייז און האַרט.
און געוואָלט האָב איך זיי וויינען דאָס מייניקע געוויין,
נאָר אויף מיר האָבן באַן און שיף געוואַרט, —
האָב איך זיי געזאָגט: אַ גוטע נאַכט, איך דאַרף שוין גיין.

נעכט אויף באַנען. טעג אויף שיפן. וואַסער. שטויב.
גרויע בערד צעשויבערט הוידען זיך אויף שטריק.
איך — אין ווינט פון ים, צי ביי אַ לויפנדיקער שויב, —
הער, ווי מיינע בייזע פעטערס רופן מיך צוריק.

*Hob ikh oysgetapt di berd: groy un beyz un hart.*
*Un gevolt hob ikh zey veynen dos maynike geveyn,*
*nor oyf mir hobn ban un shif gevart, —*
*hob ikh zey gezogt: a gute nakht, ikh darf shoyn geyn.*

*Nekht oyf banen. Teg oyf shifn. Vaser. Shtoyb.*
*Groye berd tseshoybert hoyden zikh oyf shtrik.*
*Ikh — in vint fun yam, tsi bay a loyfndiker shoyb, —*
*her, vi mayne beyze feters rufn mikh tsurik.*

I fingered the beards: grey and fierce and hard.
And I wanted to cry out to them my own woe,
but for me train and ship were waiting,
so I said to them: Goodnight, for I must go.

Nights on trains. Days on ships. Dust. Rain.
Grey beards, unkempt, on nooses swing and slack.
In the wind at sea, or at a dripping pane,
I hear my angry uncles call me to come back.

# באַלאַדע

ער האָט נישט געמאָרדט.
ער איז געווען דער צוזאַמענטרײַבער
פֿון קינדער, מענער און ווײַבער.
ער האָט זיי בלויז געבראַכט צום אָרט.
געהערט די איילנדיקע שאָסן.
אַליין האָט ער קיין בלוט נישט פֿאַרגאָסן.
און אַז מ'האָט אים דענאַצציזירט,
האָט ער געגעבן אַ הויכן קריי
און געוואָרן גערירט.

אַ הונגעריקער געבלאָנקעט גאַנצע טעג
און געגריזשעט גראָז אויף די פֿעלדער.
אין קאָפּ בײַ אים האָבן געפֿינצטערט
אויסגעלאָשענע וועלדער.
געקומען בײַנאַכט אַהיים צום עלנדן טאַטן שווײַגן.
דער טאַטע האָט זיך געוואָלט איבערצײַגן,
צי דער זון איז נאָך אַ שטיקל מענטש.

## BALADE

*Er hot nisht gemordt.*
*Er iz geven der tsuzamentrayber*
*fun kinder, mener un vayber.*
*Er hot zey bloyz gebrakht tsum ort.*
*Gehert di aylndike shosn.*
*Aleyn hot er kayn blut nisht fargosn.*
*Un az m'hot im denatsizirt,*
*hot er gegebn a hoykhn krey*
*un gevorn gerirt.*

*A hungeriker geblonket gantse teg*
*un gegrizhet groz oyf di felder.*
*In kop bay im hobn gefintstert*
*oysgeleshene velder.*
*Gekumen baynakht aheym tsum elndn tatn shvaygn.*
*Der tate hot zikh gevolt ibertsaygn,*
*tsi der zun iz nokh a shtikl mentsh.*

# 35

## J. GLATSTEIN

### BALLAD

He did not kill.
He was the herder
of children, men, and women.
He only brought them there.
Heard the hurried shots.
He himself shed no blood.
And when he was de-Nazified
he gave a noisy crow
and grew insane.

Hungry he rambled all day
and gnawed grasses in the fields.
In his head glowered
darkened forests.
Came home at night to his lonely father and was mute
His father wanted to show himself
if his son were still a little human.

מיט די פֿאַרגעלטע הענט פֿון לעדער-פֿאַבריק
האָט טאַטע זון געשלאָגן.
געוואָרט אַז דער זון זאָל געבן קריק.
זאָל ער שרייען, זאָל ער עפּעס זאָגן.
ער האָט געפּאַטשט דאָס יונגע, פֿאַרקרענקטע פּנים,
געריסן און פֿאַרשעמט דאָס ברודיקע בערדל.
געוויינט האָט דער טאַטע.
דער זון האָט געהירזשט ווי אַ פֿערדל.

זון איז געשלאָפֿן אויף דער ערד
און געחלומט —
אַ גאַנצער וואַלד איז משוגע געוואָרן,
אויף יעדער בוים
און אויף טויזנט שרעקן.
אַלע ביימער האָבן געשריגן
און געטריבן מיט ווילדע עקן,
גרויסע, גרינע פֿליגן.

*Mit di fargelte hent fun leder-fabrik*
*hot tate zun geshlogn.*
*Gevart az der zun zol gebn krik.*
*Zol er shrayen, zol er epes zogn.*
*Er hot gepatsht dos yunge, farkrenkte ponem,*
*gerisn un farshemt dos brudike berdl.*
*Geveynt hot der tate.*
*Der zun hot gehirzht vi a ferdl.*

*Zun iz geshlofn oyf der erd*
*un gekholemt —*
*A gantser vald iz meshuge gevorn,*
*oyf yeder boym*
*un oyf toyznt shrekn.*
*Ale beymer hobn geshrign*
*un getribn mit vilde ekn,*
*groyse, grine flign.*

**35**

With his hands yellow from the leather factory
the father beat the son.
Waited for the son to hit him back.
Let him yell, let him but say something.
He slapped the young sickly face,
ripped and shamed the filthy little beard.
The father wept.
The son whinnied like a horse.

The son slept on the earth
and dreamed —
a whole wood gone crazy,
in every tree
and in a thousand fears.
Every tree screamed
and with wild tails beat away
great green flies.

ער האָט גוט געדענקט.
אים האָט איצטער גאָרנישט פֿאַרדראָסן.
ער האָט ניט געשאָסן.
ער האָט בלויז געלאַכט און ארויסגעטריבן
ייִדן, ייִדן, ייִדן
פֿון איינגעפֿאַלענע שטיבן,
פֿון באַהעלטענישן אין פֿינצטערע חורבות.

אַ יונג מיידל האָט געהונקען.
איין פֿוס איז ביי איר געווען באַשוכט,
דער צווייטער באָרוועס.
אַן אַלטער, פֿאַרשעמטער ייִד,
וואָס אויף אים האָט ער מיט געוואַלט ארויפֿגעוואָרפֿן
אַ ווייבעריש קליידל,
האָט געוויינט און געפֿירט ביים האַנט דאָס מיידל.

*Er hot gut gedenkt.*
*Im hot itster gornisht fardrosn.*
*Er hot nisht geskosn.*
*Er hot bloyz gelakht un aroysgetribn*
*yidn, yidn, yidn*
*fun ayngefalene shtibn,*
*fun baheltenishn in finstere khurves.*

*A yung meydl hot gehunken.*
*Eyn fus iz bay ir geven bashukht,*
*der tsveyter borves.*
*An alter, farshemter yid,*
*vos oyf im hot er mit gvalt aroyfgevorfn*
*a vayberish kleydl,*
*hot geveynt un gefirt baym hant dos meydl.*

He remembered well.
He was not sorry now.
He had not fired.
He had only laughed and driven
Jews, Jews, Jews
from collapsing hovels,
from hiding places in dark ruins.

A young girl limped.
One of her feet was shod,
the other bare.
An old humiliated Jew
that he had forced to wear
a woman's dress
wept and led the girl by the hand.

שפעטער האָט ער אויסגעזוכט די צוויי קאָמישע יידן,
געזעסן לעבן זיי, געגרויכערט פּאַפּיראָסן.
אָבער ער איז געווען מוראדיק צופרידן.
ער האָט זיי נישט געשאָסן,
פונווייטנס האָבן געפינצטערט פאַרלאָשענע שטובן.
ער איז געווען מוראדיק צופרידן.


און איינמאָל אין אַ פרימאָרגן,
ווען דער טאַטע איז אַוועק אין פֿאַבריק
האָט ער אויסגעזוכט אין סטעליע אַ זיכערן טשוואָק,
געפונען אַ בענקל,
פֿאַרוואָרפֿן אויפֿן האַלדז אַ שטריק.
מער האָט ער שוין נישט געקאָנט פֿאַרטראָגן.
ער איז געהאַנגען, געשפּירט ווי גיך ער לויפֿט.
איצט האָט ער געהירזשעט און געלאַכט.


זאָל אים דאָס מיידל מיטן באַרוועסן פֿוס,
און מיטן ווייבערשן קליידל דער אַלטער ייד
פּרואוון דעריאָגן.


Shpeter hot er oysgezukht di tsvey komishe yidn,
gezesn lebn zey, geroykhert papirosn.
Ober er iz geven moyredik tsefridn.
Er hot zey nisht geshosn,
funvaytns hobn gefintstert farloshene shtubn.
Er iz geven moyredik tsufridn.

Un eynmol in a frimorgn,
ven der tate iz avek in fabrik
hot er oysgezukht in stelye a zikhern tshvok,
gefunen a benkl,
farvorfn oyfn haldz a shtrik.
Mer hot er es shoyn nisht gekont fartrogn.
Er is gehangen, geshpirt vi gikh er loyft.
Itst hot er gehirzhet un gelakht.

Zol im dos meydl mitn borvesn fus,
un mitn vayberishn kleydl der alter yid
pruvn deryogn.

Later he hunted up the two comical Jews,
sat near them, smoked cigarettes.
But he was appallingly pleased.
He had not shot them,
far away extinguished houses darkened.
He was appallingly pleased.

And once upon a morning,
when the father left for the factory,
he hunted out a sound nail in the ceiling,
found a bench,
threw a rope around his neck.
He could not endure anymore.
He hung, felt how fast he ran.
Now he whinnied and he laughed.

Now let that girl with the one bare foot,
and the old Jew in the woman's dress
just try to catch him.

# אומעטום

מגדל דוד, כינעזישע מויער —
אומעטום דערזעלבער טרויער.

פירענייזן, הרי יהודה —
אומעטום אַ לעצטע סעודה.

ביי ירדן, דניעפּער, דאָניי, טיבער
טראָגט זיך אונדזער קלאָג בצינבור.

טויט-גרימאַסע אין יעדן שפּיגל.
בלוט פון קינדער אין יעדן ציגל.

אַ קרבן ברענט אין יעדן פייער.
אויף יעדן בוים הענגט אַ באַפרייער.

## UMETUM

*Migdal Dovid, Khinezishe moyer —*
*umetum derzelber troyer.*

*Pireneyzn, Hori Yehude —*
*umetum a letste sude.*

*Bay Yarden, Dnyeper, Donay, Tiber*
*trogt zikh undzer klog betsiber.*

*Toyt-grimase in yedn shpigl.*
*Blut fun kinder in yedn tsigl.*

*A korbn brent in yedn fayer.*
*Oyf yedn boym hengt a bafrayer.*

# 36

## A. ALMI

### EVERYWHERE

Tower of David, Chinese wall —
the selfsame sorrow over all.

Hills of Judea, the Pyrenees,
the Last Supper ubiquitous.

At the Jordan, Danube, Tiber, Dnieper,
our lamentation moves together.

In every mirror death grimace,
children's blood in every place.

A victim burns in every fire.
On every tree hangs a Messiah.

I BURN AND I BURN
AND I AM NOT CONSUMED

H. Leivick's "Forever," a lovely song in its musical setting and especially popular in the 1940's, stresses the sadness and the necessity of the long road Yiddish poets, and Jews in general, have walked and are prepared, unwillingly, to walk again. The same sense of *déjà vu* is present in the entire group. Chaim Grade, member of the younger group of Polish poets, presents "In Wolfen Teeth" as a private groan and "The Road of Suffering" as a more objective lament on Ezekiel's lips. Einhorn and Sutskever feel alienated and abandoned by the world, and Sutskever can see no solution to his lonely role as one of the few survivors of the Nazi terror. His poem "How?" was written in the Vilna Ghetto, February 14, 1943. Glatstein speaks in his pose of poet and mourns the humiliation and corruption of the Yiddish creative spirit in our day. His poem, like Kulbak's, offers the catalogue of sorrows from which the Yiddish poet must select his subject matter and his attitude. Zeitlin finds an ambivalent salvation in death, and Kadie Molodowsky is stubbornly defiant. Her world, the world of the Yiddish poet, is geographically large, but its metaphors are restricted, limited by the boundaries of the heart.

# אייביק

די וועלט נעמט מיך ארום מיט שטעכיקע הענט,
און טראָגט מיך צום פייער, און טראָגט מיך צום שייטער;
איך ברען און איך ברען און איך ווער ניט פארברענט, —
איך הייב זיך אויף ווידער און שפאן אַוועק ווייטער.

איך שפאַן דורך פאַבריקן און פאַל אונטער ראָד,
איך רייס־אויף די דאַמפן מיט קראַפט מיט באַנייטער,
איך לייג זיך אַוועק, ווי אַ נייער יסוד, —
איך הייב זיך אויף ווידער און שפאַן אַוועק ווייטער.

אָט שפאַן איך זיך איין אין געשפאַן פון אַ פּערד,
און איבער מיר בייטשט אַ דערצאָרנטער רייטער;
ווי אַן אַקער אַ שאַרפער איך גראָב דורך די ערד, —
איך הייב זיך אויף ווידער און שפאַן אַוועק ווייטער.


*EYBIK*

*Di velt nemt mikh arum mit shtekhike hent,*
*un trogt mikh tsum fayer, un trogt mikh tsum shayter;*
*ikh bren un ikh bren un ikh ver nit farbrent, —*
*ikh heyb zikh oyf vider un shpan avek vayter.*

*Ikh shpan durkh fabrikn un fal unter rod,*
*ikh rays oyf di damfn mit kraft mit banayter,*
*ikh leyg zikh avek, vi a nayer yesod, —*
*ikh heyb zikh oyf vider un shpan avek vayter.*

*Ot shpan ikh zikh ayn in geshpan fun a ferd,*
*un iber mir baytsht a dertsornter rayter;*
*vi an aker a sharfer ikh grob durkh di erd, —*
*ikh heyb zikh oyf vider un shpan avek vayter.*

# 37

# H. LEIVICK

## FOREVER

The world grasps me in hands that wound,
and bears me to fire, and bears me to auto-da-fé;
I burn and I burn, and I am not consumed.
I rise up again and go on my way.

I walk through factories and fall under wheels,
I split open machines with the strength of fresh day;
like new building ground, I lie prone under heels.
I rise up again and go on my way.

I harness myself in the gear of a horse,
and over me lashes a rider in rage;
like a sharpened plow through the earth I course.
I rise up again and go on my way.

איך זיי מײַנע לידער, ווי קערנער מען זייט,
זיי שפּראָצן, זיי וואַקסן, ווי זאַנגען און קרײַטער;
און איך אַליין ליג ווי אַ דאָרן פֿאַרדרייט, —
איך הייב זיך אויף ווידער און שפּאַן אַוועק ווײַטער.

איך וואוין אין אַ תפֿיסה.  איך רײַס אויף די צעל,
עס טרעט איבער מיר צו זײַן גליק דער באַפֿרײַטער,
און מיך לאָזט ער ליגן אין בלוט בײַ דער שוועל, —
איך הייב זיך אויף ווידער און שפּאַן אַוועק ווײַטער.

אין בלוט מײַנע קליידער, — די פֿיס קוים איך שלעפּ,
איך קום מיט אַ ליבשאַפֿט פֿון לעצטן געלײַטער;
איך קום צו אַ שטיבל, איך פֿאַל אויף די טרעפּ — — —
איך הייב זיך אויף ווידער און שפּאַן אַוועק ווײַטער.

*Ikh zey mayne lider, vi kerner men zeyt,*
*zey shprotsn, zey vaksn, vi zangn un krayter;*
*un ikh aleyn lig vi a dorn fardreyt, —*
*ikh heyb zikh oyf vider un shpan avek vayter.*

*Ikh voyn in a tfise. Ikh rays oyf di tsel,*
*es tret iber mir tsu zayn glik der bafrayter,*
*un mikh lozt er lign in blut bay der shvel, —*
*ikh heyb zikh oyf vider un shpan avek vayter.*

*In blut mayne kleyder, — di fis koym ikh shlep,*
*ikh kum mit a libshaft fun letstn gelayter;*
*ikh kum tsu a shtibl, ikh fal oyf di trep — — —*
*ikh heyb zikh oyf vider un shpan avek vayter.*

**37**

I sow my songs as kernels are sown;
they shoot up, they flourish, like cornstalks and hay;
but I, like a twisted thorn, lie alone.
I rise up again and go on my way.

I live in a prison. I break open the door,
the freed man treads on me to meet his glad fate,
and leaves me lying in blood on the floor.
I rise up again and go on my way.

My clothing bloodied — my feet can scarce crawl,
I come with love of anguished yesterdays;
I come to a hovel, on its steps I fall.
I rise up again and go on my way.

# אויסלייז

פעלדגריל האמערט: גיי׳מיר, גיי׳מיר.
מידע ביימער — זון דערברענט.
ס׳אויג דיינס פלעמלט. שלעפריק דרעמלט
שוואכער ווינט אויף דיינע הענט,
ס׳פאלט אָט באלד די נאכט — און דעמולט? ...


ווייטע לאָנקע, טונקל גרינט זי.
גאָט, גיי אויף אין אונדזער מיט.
זעסט? דאָרט שטייט דער טויט. אַהינצו
לאָמיר צוגיין זאלבעדריט.
ער, דער פערטער וויל אונדז בענטשן.


דאָרט אין סידור פון די שאָטנס
גליען נייע שטיקער טראָף.
שוואַרץ־טאָפאָליש שטאַרט דער פערטער,
ער, דער זין פון דיין באַשאַף.
לידער שטאַרבן, ס׳פלאַצן ווערטער.


## OYSLEYZ

*Feldgril hamert: gey'mir, gey'mir.*
*Mide beymer — zun derbrent.*
*S'oyg dayns flemlt. Shlefrik dremlt*
*shvakher vint oyf dayne hent,*
*s'falt ot bald di nakht — un demolt? . . .*

*Vayte lonke, tunkl grint zi.*
*Got, gey oyf in undzer mit.*
*Zest? Dort shteyt der toyt. Ahintsu*
*lomir tsugeyn zalbedrit.*
*Er, der ferter vil undz bentshn.*

*Dort in sidur fun di shotns*
*gliyen naye shtiker traf.*
*Shvarts-topolish shtart der ferter,*
*er, der zin fun dayn bashaf.*
*Lider shtarbn. S'platsn verter.*

**38**

# AARON ZEITLIN

## SALVATION

Field cricket hammers: Go on, go on.
Tired trees burn in sun.
Your eye flames. A frail wind
dreams sleepy in your hand.
Soon night will fall — and then?

Far meadow, darkly greening.
God, rise up, in our midst be.
You see? There stands Death. There
let us go, all three.
He, the Fourth, wants to bless us.

There in the prayer book of shadows
a new alphabet is gleaming.
Doubly black arises the Fourth,
he, Your creation's meaning.
Songs die. Words explode.

# אין וועלפישע ציין

איך טראָג אום מיין שעפסענעם לעבן אין וועלפישע ציין,
איך לעב ווי אַ שעפס און האָב פיינט ווי אַ וואָלף זיך אַליין.
עס גייען אַוועק מיינע וואָכן ווי האָלצהעקקער מיד,
און לאָזן די העק אין מיין קראַנקן געמיט.
עס קומען מחשבות צו מיר ווי אבלים פון פעלד, —
זעצן זיך שבעה אַוועק אויפן גורל פון וועלט.
און ווי מען נעמט איבער אַ קינד פון די הענט
אויף אַ לייטער, געשטעלט ביי אַ פענסטער, וואָס ברענט,
אַזוי גיבן איבער די שלאָפלאָזע נעכט מיינע טעג,
אַז איך וויל ווי אַ וואָלף פון אַ שטייג אין די וועלדער אַוועק.
נאַכט קלינגען אין מיר שניי־באַדעקטע קופאָלן אַ סך,
זיי שרייען ווי פייגל אויף נאַקעטע פעלדער: זיי וואַך!
וואַך איך און מיין: ס'גייט די וועלט שוין אַראָפּ פון איר קרייץ . . .
ביז פינסטערניש גיט אויף מיין האָפענונג ווידער אַ פלייץ — — —
און איך זע אין מיין שוואַכקייט דעם פיין פון מיין דור און זיין שאַנד
און איך האָב זיך פיינט, ווי אַ מאַן זיין פאַרטריקנטע האַנט . . .

## IN VELFISHE TSEYN

*Ikh trog um mayn shepsenem lebn in velfishe tseyn,*
*ikh leb vi a sheps un hob faynt vi a volf zikh aleyn.*
*Es geyen avek mayne vokhn vi holtsheker mid,*
*un lozn di hek in mayn krankn gemit.*
*Es kumen makhshoves tsu mir vi aveylim fun feld, —*
*zetsn zikh shive avek oyfn goyrl fun velt.*
*Un vi men nemt iber a kind fun di hent*
*oyf a leyter, geshtelt bay a fenster, vos brent,*
*azoy gibn iber di shlofloze nekht mayne teg,*
*az ikh vil vi a volf fun a shtayg in di velder avek.*
*Nakht klingen in mir shney-badekte kupoln a sakh,*
*zay shrayen vi feygl oyf nakete felder: zay vakh!*
*Vakh ikh un meyn: s'geyt di velt shoyn arop fun ir*
*    krayts . . .*
*biz finsternish git oyf mayn hofenung vider a flayts — — —*
*un ikh ze in mayn shvakhkayt dem payn fun mayn dor*
*    un zayn shand*
*un ikh hob zikh faynt, vi a man zayn fartriknte hant . . .*

# 39

# CHAIM GRADE

## IN WOLFEN TEETH

I carry my sheepish life about in the teeth of a wolf,
I live like a sheep and like a wolf hate myself.
Exhausted woodcutters, my weeks depart,
leave their axes in my ailing heart.
Mourners from the field, my thoughts emerge,
for the fate of the world, they sing their dirge.
And just as a child is taken from hands
at a burning window where a ladder stands,
so the sleepless nights hand over my every day,
and I must run, like a wolf from his cage, to the forest
    away.
Within me at night many snow-covered cupolas toll:
Stay awake! like birds on naked fields they call.
I wake and believe: the world from her cross descends . . .
until darkness blots up my hopes again.
And I see in my weakness the sorrow of my time and its
    shame,
and I hate myself, like a man whose own hand has grown
    lame.

# װער ציט מיר דען זײן אָרעם אױם

װער ציט מיר דען זײן אָרעם אױם
מיט זון אין בליק?
װער שליסט מיר אױפֿן שװאָרצן תהום
אַ גאָלדן בריק?
װער האָט מיט מיר אין שטומער נאַכט
אַ װאָרט גערעדט?
און װער דערמאָנט מײן נאָמען שטיל
אין זײן געבעט?
די טירן שטײען אַלע פֿעסט פֿאַרמאַכט;
דער שלאָפֿלאָזער װאַכט אָפּ אַלײן זײן נאַכט;
דער קראַנקער ליגט אַלײן געשמידט צום בעט,
און יעדער מורמלט פֿאַר זיך זײן געבעט.
אָ, טריט געטראָטענע אין זאַמד פֿון װײטן װײט! ..
אָ, טריט פֿאַרשאָטענע אין װיסטער אײנזאַמקײט! ..

# VER TSIT MIR DEN ZAYN OREM OYS

*Ver tsit mir den zayn orem oys*
*mit zun in blik?*
*Ver shlist mir oyfn shvartsn tehom*
*a goldn brik?*
*Ver hot mit mir in shtumer nakht*
*a vort geredt?*
*Un ver dermont mayn nomen shtil*
*in zayn gebet?*
*Di tirn shteyen ale fest farmakht;*
*der shloflozer vakht op aleyn zayn nakht;*
*der kranker ligt aleyn geshmidt tsum bet,*
*un yeder murmlt far zikh zayn gebet.*
*O, trit getrotene in zamd fun vaytn vayt! ..*
*O, trit farshotene in vister aynzamkayt! ..*

# 40

# DAVID EINHORN

## WHO THEN EXTENDS HIS ARMS TO ME

Who then extends his arms to me,
with sun in his glance?
Who bridges over the black abyss for me
with a golden span?
Who has in the muffled night
said a word to me?
And who has recalled my name
in his quiet plea?
The doors are all standing shut tight;
the insomniac watches alone all night;
the invalid, welded to his bed, lies alone,
and each man murmurs his prayers on his own.
O footsteps trod in sand of far farness!
O footsteps erased in dry loneliness!

אויף אַלע גרינע בוימער זינגען
פייגל פיל;
אין יעדער שפּאַלט און שפּעלטל גרילט
פֿאַר זיך אַ גריל;
פֿאַרבענקטע שטימען רופֿן, שרייען
אָן אַ צאָל,
נאָר קיינער האָט קיין ענטפֿער
אויף זיין קול.
דער טויבער הערט זיין אייגן שוויגן שטום;
דער בלינדער זעט זיין שוואַרצע נאַכט אַרום;
און יעדער איינער זיין שטערנדל פֿאַרמאָגט.
און יעדן איינציקן זיין טיפֿער טרויער נאָגט.
אַ, טרערן מענטשלעכע אין אָפּגרונט פֿון דער צייט! ..
אַ, בערגלעך זאַמדיקע אין וויסטער איינזאַמקייט! ..

Oyf ale grine boymer zingen
feygl fil;
in yeder shpalt un shpeltl grilt
far zikh a gril;
farbenkte shtimen rufn, shrayen
on a tsol,
nor keyner hot kayn entfer
oyf zayn kol.
Der toyber hert zayn eygn shvaygn shtum;
der blinder zet zayn shvartse nakht arum;
un yeder eyner zayn shterndl farmogt,
un yedn eyntsikn zayn tifer troyer nogt.
O, trern mentshlekhe in opgrunt fun der tsayt! ..
O, berglekh zamdike in vister aynzamkayt! ..

**40**

On all the green trees
many birds twitter;
in all cracks and crannies
crickets chitter;
unnumbered lonely voices
shout, cajole,
but no one has an answer
to his call.
The deaf man hears his own dumbness sound,
the blind man sees his black night all round,
and each man has a star of his own,
and each man nurses his deep woe alone.
O human tears in the time's abyss!
O sandy mounds in dry loneliness!

מיר אַלע וואַנדערן ביינאַנד
אין כישוף־לאַנד,
צווישן יעדן שטייט אַ קאַלט
קרישטאָלן וואַנט,
אומזיסט דאָס שרייען, רופן, ברעכן
מיט געוואַלד, —
די טויבע וואַנט בלייבט אייביק
דורכזיכטיק און קאַלט.
דער הימל אויבן איז נאָר אָפן ווייט,
און אונטער אים אין טיפער איינזאַמקייט
ליגט יעדערן זיין טונקעלער וועג צעשפרייט, —
דער בעטלער שרייט,
דער קיניג שווייגט און גייט . . .

*Mir ale vandern baynand*
*in kishef-land,*
*tsvishn yedn shteyt a kalt*
*krishtoln vant,*
*umzist dos shrayen, rufn, brekhn*
*mit gevalt, —*
*di toybe vant blaybt eybik*
*durkhzikhtik un kalt.*
*Der himl oybn iz nor ofn vayt,*
*un unter im in tifer aynzamkayt*
*ligt yedern zayn tunkeler veg tseshpreyt, —*
*der betler shrayt,*
*der kinig shvaygt un geyt. . .*

**40**

We all roam together
in magic land.
Between each of us a cold
crystal wall stands.
Useless to smash by force,
shout or dissent —
the deaf wall stands forever
cold, transparent.
Only the sky above is open, wide,
and under it in deep isolation
each man's darkened road is spread.
The beggar shouts,
the king is mute and strides ahead.

# שטילער, שטילער

שטילער! שטילער! רעדט ניט הויך!
שטײט געבױגען שװאַרץ און בלײך.
אײנגעבױגענע אין פּײן,
שװײגט און האַלט דעם אָטעם אײן.

פֿון דער טיפֿער נאַכט אַרױס
און פֿון קײנעם ניט געהערט,
װעט ער אױף אַ װײַסן פֿערד
קומען שטיל צו אונזער הױז.

פֿון זײן לױטערען געזיכט
און זײן קלאָרען װײַסען קלײד
װעיען װעט אױף אונז די פֿרײד,
פֿאַלן װעט אױף אונז זײן ליכט.

## SHTILER, SHTILER

*Shtiler! shtiler! redt nit hoykh!*
*Shteyt geboygn shvarts un bleykh.*
*Ayngeboygene in payn,*
*shvaygt un halt dem otem ayn.*

*Fun der tifer nakht aroys*
*un fun keynem nit gehert,*
*vet er oyf a vaysn ferd*
*kumen shtil tsu undzer hoyz.*

*Fun zayn loytern gezikht*
*un zayn kloren, vaysn kleyd*
*veyen vet oyf undz di frevd,*
*faln vet oyf undz zayn likht.*

# 41

## MANI LEIB

### BE STILL

Be still, be still, don't speak out loud.
Bleak and pale now stand bowed.
Bowed down in pain,
be dumb, your breath restrain.

Out of the deepening night,
when no one can hear,
at our house he will appear
on a steed of white.

His garments clear and white,
and his glowing face,
will be his glad embrace,
will fold us in his light.

זײַט נאָר שטילער! רעדט ניט הויך!
שטעהט געבויגן שװאַרץ און בלײך.
אײַנגעבויגענע אין פּײַן,
שטייט און האַלט דעם אָטעם אײַן.

אויב מען האָט אונז אָפּגענאַרט,
און מען האָט אונז אויסגעלאַכט,
און די גאַנצע, לאַנגע נאַכט
האָבן מיר אומזיסט געװאַכט,

װעלען מיר אין אונזער בראָך
בויגען זיך צום האַרטען דיל
און מיר װעלן שװײַגן שטיל,
שטילער נאָך און שטילער נאָך.

*Zayt nor shtiler! redt nit hoykh!*
*shteyt geboygn shvarts un bleykh.*
*Ayngeboygene in payn,*
*shteyt un halt dem otem ayn.*

*Oyb men hot undz opgenart,*
*un men hot undz oysgelakht,*
*un di gantse lange nakht*
*hobn mir umzist gevakht,*

*veln mir in undzer brokh*
*boygn zikh tsum hartn dil*
*un mir veln shvaygn shtil,*
*shtiler nokh un shtiler nokh.*

**41**

Only be still, don't speak out loud.
Bleak and pale now stand bowed.
Bowed down in pain,
stand, your breath restrain.

If we have been duped,
made laughingstock again,
and have watched in vain
through the whole long night —

we will in our adversity
bow down to the hard, hard floor
and we will speak no more,
stiller yet and stiller be.

זייט זשע שטילער! רעדט ניט הויך!
שטײט געבויגן שװארץ און בלײך.
איינגעבויגענע אין פײן,
שטײט און האלט דעם אטעם אײן.

*Zayt zhe shtiler! redt nit hoykh!*
*Shteyt geboygn shvarts un bleykh.*
*Ayngeboygene in payn,*
*shteyt un halt dem otem ayn.*

**41**

Then be still, don't speak out loud.
Bleak and pale now stand bowed.
Bowed down in pain,
stand, your breath restrain.

# דער וועג פון פיין

א, גאָט, איך בין בײַ דיר אין האַנט — אַ שוואַרצער טאָוול,
געקריצט מיט פּייער איז אויף מיר דײַן האַס.
איך האָב אַרומגעבלאָנדזשעט בײַ די טויערן פון בבל
און אויסגערופן דיך אויף יעדער גאַס.

זיי זײַנען זיך צעלאָפן ווי די שאָטנס,
בין איך געבליבן מיט צעשפּרייטע הענט.
דער שטויב האָט ווי אַ חורבה מיך פאַרשאָטן,
דער הייסער מדבר-ווינט האָט מיך געשענדט.

אַוועקגעפלויגן זײַנען אַלע מײַנע ווערטער,
ווי זינגענדיקע פייגל פון אַ בוים.
צו דער פינסטערניש פון פאַר מײַן אָנהייב אַ צוריקגעקערטער,
האָב איך געשוויגן ווי אַ בערגל ליים.

*DER VEG FUN PAYN*

*(Fun Yekhezkl)*

*O, got, ikh bin bay dir in hant — a shvartser tovl,*
*gekritst mit fayer iz oyf mir dayn has.*
*Ikh hob arumgeblondzhet bay di toyern fun bovl*
*un oysgerufn dikh oyf yeder gas.*

*Zey zaynen zikh tselofn vi di shotns,*
*bin ikh geblibn mit tseshpreyte hent.*
*Der shtoyb hot vi a khurve mikh farshotn,*
*der heyser midbor-vint hot mikh geshendt.*

*Avekgefloygen zaynen ale mayne verter,*
*vi zingendike feygl fun a boym.*
*Tsu der finsternish fun far mayn onheyb a tsurikgekerter,*
*hob ikh geshvign vi a bergl leym.*

# 42

# CHAIM GRADE

## THE ROAD OF SUFFERING
### (From Ezekiel)

O God, I am in Your hand a blackened slate;
Your hate is etched on me with fire's heat.
I have wandered at the gates of Babylon
and called to You on every street.

They scuttled off like shadows
and I was left with empty hands.
The dust settled on me, as on a ruin;
I was raped by the wind of desert sands.

Like singing birds from a tree
all my words have flown away.
Turned back to the dark of before my beginning,
I grew silent as a mound of clay.

ווי אַ מעסער אין דער ערד אַ טיף פֿאַרשטעקטער,
האָב איך אין זיך אַרײַנגעפֿינקלט און געשטומט, —
ביז דו ביסט ווידער מיר פֿאַרבײַ און אויפֿגעוועקט מיר
מיט דײַן אָטעם ווי אַ גליִקער סאַמום.

מײַן האַרץ האָט אָפּגעגעבן זיך דײַן שטורעם,
ווי עס גיט זיך אָפּ דעם ווינט — דער ים.
אָ, גאָט, איך בין פֿאַר דײַנע רייד נאָר פֿורעם,
און דו ביסט אין מײַן מויל — אַ פֿלאַם.

אַ שטויב-געווירבל איז געוואָרן פֿון מײַן קאָלטן,
אַ פֿאָכנדיקער שווערד — מײַן אויסגעשטרעקטע האַנט.
אַ וועלט האָב איך געבענטשט, אַ וועלט פֿאַרשאָלטן,
און זײַן האָב איך געוואָלט — אַ ציגל אין אַ וואַנט,

Vi a meser in der erd a tif farshtekter,
hob ikh in zikh arayngefinklt un geshtumt, —
biz du bist vider mir farbay un oyfgevekt mir
mit dayn otem vi a gliyeker samum.

Mayn harts hot opgegebn zikh dayn shturem,
vi es git zikh op dem vint — der yam.
O, got, ikh bin far dayne reyd nor furem,
un du bist in mayn moyl — a flam.

A shtoyb-gevirbl iz gevorn fun mayn koltn,
a fokhndiker shverd — mayn oysgeshtrekte hant.
A velt hob ikh gebentsht, a velt farsholtn,
un zayn hob ikh gevolt — a tsigl in a vant,

**42**

Like a knife thrust deep into the earth,
I gleamed within myself and was dumb
until again You passed and gave me birth
with Your breath, a hot simoom.

My heart surrendered to Your storm,
like wind making the sea tame.
O God, of Your words I am but the form,
and You on my lips — a flame.

My matted hair became a dust-wind swirled,
my outstretched hand — a brandished sword.
I blessed a world, I cursed a world
and wanted but to be — a brick within a wall,

אַ שטיין צווישן בלינדע שטיינער איינגעוואָקסן,
און וואָלט איך נאָך געווען אַ פֿענסטערל פֿאַר שײַן, —
איך בין געווען אַ כמאַרע פֿול מיט דונערן און שלאַקסן,
אין זיי — זיי האָבן מיר געזאָגט: אַ נביא וויל ער זײַן! ...


האָב איך פֿון זיך מײַן קלייד אַראָפּגעצויגן,
און זיי אַוועקגעשאָנקען אויך מײַן לײַב.
דער ווײַט האָב איך אַוועקגעגעבן מײַנע אויגן,
דער ערד דער זאַמדיקער — מײַן ווײַב ...


און ניט גערעדט האָב איך שוין מער אין בילדער,
איך בין אַליין געווען אַ שרעק-געשטאַלט.
אַ, גאָט, געמאַכט האָסטו מיך ווילדער
פֿון דער הונגעריקער חיה אינעם וואַלד.

*a shteyn tsvishn blinde shteyner ayngevaksn,*
*un volt ikh nokh geven a fensterl far shayn, —*
*ikh bin geven a khmare ful mit dunern un shlaksn,*
*un zey — zey hobn mir gezogt: A novi vil er zayn! ...*

*Hob ikh fun zikh mayn kleyd aropgetsoygn,*
*un zey avekgeshonken oykh mayn layb.*
*Der vayt hob ikh avekgegebn mayne oygn,*
*der erd der zamdiker — mayn vayb ...*

*Un nit geredt hob ikh shoyn mer in bilder,*
*ikh bin aleyn geven a shrek-geshtalt.*
*O, got, gemakht hostu mir vilder*
*fun der hungeriker khaye inem vald.*

**42**

a stone ingrown among blind stones;
a window for the light if I could but be —
I was a cloud of thunder and of plague
and "He wants to be a prophet!" they said to me.

Then I drew from myself my robe,
and gave them too my body's life.
My eyes I gifted to the distances,
and to the sandy earth — I gave my wife.

And I spoke no more in metaphor,
I myself a horror figure stood.
O God, You have made me wilder
than the hungry creature of the wood.

א דראָאונג איז געווען מיין שטיינערנער געלעגער,
א בייזע וואָרענונג — מיין אויסגעפֿליקטע באָרד,
איך בין געווען אַליין געיאָגטער און אויך יעגער;
מיין ברויט מיט מיסט — דאָס שוידערלעכסטע וואָרט.

האָבן זיי זיך ביי די טויערן געקליבן,
אין זייער חזק האָט געשוימט דער האַס:
— קומט, לאָמיר זען, וואָס ער האָט מיט די נעגל אָנגעשריבן
אויף זיין ברוסט אין רויטער משוגעת...

אין רינג פֿון זייערע געזיכטער האָב איך אויפֿגעשטורעמט ווידער, —
נאָר באַלד האָב איך אין זיי דערקענט — די שלאַנג,
וואָס האָט אַרויסגעפּויזעט פֿון דער טיף צו הערן לידער —
מיין יאָמער איז געווען פֿאַר זיי געזאַנג.

*A droung iz geven mayn shteynerner geleger,*
*a beyze vorenung — mayn oysgeflikte bord,*
*ikh bin geven aleyn geyogter un oykh yeger;*
*mayn broyt mit mist — dos shoyderlekhste vort.*

*Hobn zey zikh bay di toyern geklibn,*
*in zeyer khoyzik hot geshoymt der has:*
*— Kumt, lomir zen, vos er hot mit di negl ongeshribn*
*oyf zayn brust in royter mishegas ...*

*In ring fun zeyere gezikhter hob ikh oyfgeshturemt*
*vider, —*
*nor bald hob ikh in zey derkent — di shlang,*
*vos hot aroysgepoyzet fun der tif tsu hern lider —*
*mayn yomer iz geven far zey gezang.*

My stony litter was a menace,
an evil warning — my plucked-out beard,
I was both hunted and the hunter,
my bread of offal — the word most feared.

Then they gathered together at the gates,
hate foamed in their mocking jest;
"Come — let's see what he's written with his nails
in reddened madness on his breast. . . "

In the circle of their faces I stormed out again —
but soon I recognized them — the snake
that had crawled from the depths to hear songs —
my lamentation for a song they take.

און איך בין דורך דעם פיין פון אַלע פּיינען:
מיין שליחות איז געווען פאַר זיי אַ ליד. —
איצט הער איך שוין ניט מער מיין ווייטאָג טענהן,
איך גיי אויף דערנער און עס זינגען מיינע טריט.

איך גיי דעם וועג, וואָס איך האָב אויסגעטראָטן,
און קלאָגט זיך, ווי אַ קינד, ביים וועג — אַ שטיין,
טיילט אָפּ זיך פון מיין גוף און דעקט אים צו — אַ שאָטן . . .
און ווייטער טראָג איך מיין געלייטערטן געביין.

פאַרנאַכט, עס יאָמערן אין מדבר די שאַקאַלן,
איך נעם די שקיעה ווי אַ פייגעלע אין מיינע הענט. —
אַ, גאָט, מוז אייביק זיין באַפאַלענע און וואָס באַפאַלן?
פאַרוואָס האָסטו פון אונדז זיך אָפּגעווענדט?

Un ikh bin durkh dem payn fun ale paynen:
mayn shlikhes iz geven far zey a lid. —
Itst her ikh shoyn nit mer mayn veytog taynen,
ikh gey oyf derner un es zingen mayne trit.

Ikh gey dem veg, vos ikh hob oysgetrotn,
un klogt zikh, vi a kind, baym veg — a shteyn,
teylt op zikh fun mayn guf un dekt im tsu — a shotn . . .
un vayter trog ikh mayn gelaytertn gebeyn.

Farnakht, es yomern in midbor di shakaln,
ikh nem di shkiye vi a feygele in mayne hent. —
O, got, muz eybik zayn bafalene un vos bafaln?
Farvos hostu fun undz zikh opgevendt?

אמאל האט מיך צו אייך די שנאה, מיינע ברידער,
פארטעמפט, איך זאָל ניט פילן אייער פיין,
איצט לאָזט מיר ניט מיין גרויסע ליבשאַפט ווידער
ווערן — וואָס איך קען פאר אייך ניט זיין . . .

איך גיי מיין וועג — און ווען מיר וועלן זיך געפינען,
וועט ווי גאָלד אַ קלונג טאָן אונדזער פרייד,
פאראייניקן וועט אונדז דער הימל פון באגינען,
און איך וועל אָנטאָן, בענטשנדיק, מיין לייוונטענע קלייד.

**42**

h tsu aykh di sine, mayne brider,
zol nit filn ayer payn,
it mayn groyse libshaft vider
h ken far aykh nit zayn . . .

veg — un ven mir veln zikh gefinen,
klung ton undzer freyd,
undz der himl fun baginen,
on, bentshndik, mayn layvntene kleyd.

And I endured the torment of all torments:
for them a melody the message that I bring.
Now I hear no longer my pain's pleading,
I walk on thorns and my footsteps sing.

I follow the road that I have worn out,
and if on the way there weeps like a child — a stone,
a shadow parts from my body and covers it . . .
and I carry further my suffering bones.

At twilight jackals howl in the desert,
I hold in my hands, like a small bird, the sunset ray.
O God, must there always be attackers and attacked?
Why have You turned from us away?

אין טאָרבע טראָג איך אום מײן חלום,
וואָס איך האָב אויפגעהויבן פון דעם שטויב.
בין איך דען בלויז אַ משל — און משלים
זײנען אויך דער שפּאַרבער און די טויב? ...

עס מאָנט דערלייזונג אויך די בלוטדאָרשטיקע סטײע,
דער שעפּס לאָזט זיך צערײסן, נאָר ער וואַרט
אויף דער פאַרויסגעזאָגטער צײט, ווען ס'וועט די חיה
אים נעמען אויף איר רוקן מילד און צאַרט.

די אויסגעבענקטע שעה פון אויסלײזונג מוז קומען. —
וואָס וועט אָבער ווערן מיט דעם בלוט
דעם אומשולדיקן, וואָס די ערד האָט צוגענומען
דורך אַלע דורות ביז אָט דער מינוט? ...

*In torbe trog ikh um mayn kholem,*
*vos ikh hob oyfgehoybn fun dem shtoyb.*
*Bin ikh den bloyz a moshl — un mesholem*
*zaynen oykh der shparber un di toyb? ...*

*Es mont derleyzung oykh di blutdurshtike staye,*
*der sheps lozt zich tseraysn, nor er vart*
*oyf der faroysgezogter tsayt, ven s'vet di khaye*
*im nemen oyf ir rukn mild un tsart.*

*Di oysgebenkte sho fun oysleyzung muz kumen. —*
*Vos vet ober vern mit dem blut*
*dem unshuldikn, vos di erd hot tsugenumen*
*durkh ale doyres biz ot der minut? ...*

In my sack I carry around my dr
that from the dust I lifted up ab
Am I but a parable — and paral
as well the sparrow hawk and do

The bloodthirsty flock demands
the sheep let themselves be torn,
the prophesied time, when the w
take them on her back, mild and

The yearned-for hour of delivera
But what will happen to the bloo
the innocent blood the earth has
through all generations to this ve

*Amol hot*
*fartempt,*
*itst lozt m*
*vern — ve*

*Ikh gey m*
*vet vi gol*
*fareynikn*
*un ikh ve*

**42**

Once my hatred for you, brothers,
dulled me, that I might not feel your misery;
now my great love does not let me become —
that which for you I cannot be . . .

I go my way — when we will find each other
like gold our joy will sound.
We will be joined by a morning sky
and I will don, saying grace, my linen gown.

# ווי אַזוי?

ווי אַזוי און מיט וואָס וועסטו פילן
דיין בעכער אין טאָג פון באַפרייאונג?
ביסטו גרייט אין דיין פרייד צו דערפילן
דיין פאַרגאַנגענהייטס פינצטמערע שרייאונג
וואו עס גליווערן שאַרבנס פון טעג
אין אַ תהום אָן אַ גרונט, אָן אַ דעק?

## VI AZOY?

*Vi azoy un mit vos vestu filn*
*dayn bekher in tog fun bafrayung?*
*Bistu greyt in dayn freyd tsu derfiln*
*dayn fargangenhayts fintstere shrayung*
*vu es glivern sharbns fun teg*
*in a tehom on a grunt, on a dek?*

# 43

# ABRAHAM SUTSKEVER

## HOW?

How and with what will you fill
your cup on the day of release?
In your joy, are you ready to listen still
to your yesterday's black shrieks
where shards of days shudder in spasm
in a bottomless, roofless chasm?

דו וועסט זוכן אַ שליסל צו פּאַסן
פֿאַר דיינע פֿאַרהאַקטע שלעסער.
ווי ברויט וועסטו בייסן די גאַסן
און טראַכטן: דער פֿריער איז בעסער.
און די צייט וועט דיך עקבערן שטיל
ווי אין פֿויסט אַ געפֿאַנגענע גריל.

און ס'וועט זיין דיין זכרון געגליכן
צו אַן אַלטער פֿאַרשאָטענער שטאָט.
און דיין דרויסיקער בליק וועט דאָרט קריכן
ווי אַ קראָט, ווי אַ קראָט — — — — —

*Du vest zukhn a shlisl tsu pasn*
*far dayne farhakte shleser.*
*Vi broyt vestu baysn di gasn*
*un trakhtn: der friyer iz beser.*
*Un di tsayt vet dikh ekbern shtil*
*vi in foyst a gefangene gril.*

*Un s'vet zayn dayn zikorn geglikhn*
*tsu an alter farshotener shtot.*
*Un dayn droysiker blik vet dort krikhn*
*vi a krot, vi a krot — — — — —*

**43**

You will seek a key, instead,
to fit your shattered locks.
You will bite the streets like bread
and think: Earlier was better.
And the time will quietly persist
like a cricket closed in your fist.

And your memory will be compared
to an old and buried town,
and your outward vision like a mole
will burrow, dig down . . .

# ייִדישקייט

נאָך יענע שבת-לעכט, וואָס פֿלעמלען
אין דײַן זיכרון,
און זײַנען שוין באַלד געוואָרן צוקאָפּנס-ליכטער,
בײַ אַ ווײַנענדיקער נשמה,
בענקסטו אפֿשר, ייִדישער דיכטער?
פֿאַרגעס, זיי זײַנען נישט מער,
ווי טריפֿנדיקער רחמנות.

## YIDISHKAYT

*Nokh yene shabes-lekht, vos flemlen*
*in dayn zikorn,*
*un zaynen shoyn bald gevorn tsukopns-likhter,*
*bay a veynendiker neshome,*
*benkstu efsher, yidisher dikhter?*
*Farges, zey zaynen nisht mer,*
*vi trifndiker rakhmones.*

# 44

## J. GLATSTEIN

## JEWISHNESS

For those Sabbath lights that flame
in your memory
and have already become deathbed candles set
beside a weeping soul,
do you yearn perhaps, Jewish poet?
Forget it, they are no more,
like raining mercy.

א װייטיק צוצוקוקן װי פֿון ייִדישקייט
איז געװאָרן נישט מער װי חזנות,
און אויסגעטריקנט איז דער קװאָל
פֿון גאַנצן ליכטיקן ריטואַל.
זאָל פֿון ייִדישקייט װערן
בלויז אַ פֿאָלקס-ליד,
װאָס גיט אַ כאַפּ ביים האַרצן
און גיסט אָן מיט װאַרעמען האָניק
פֿון דערמאָנונג די געדערעם?
ליבערשט נעם אַזאַ יום טוב און פֿאַרשטער אים.
דו, ייִדישער דיכטער, װאָס ביסט געװאָרן די בין,
און שטעלסט צו דעם האָניק-מאַרגאַרין,
װאָס איז מוציא מיט געזאַנג.
נישט מער װי אַ משורר ביסטו,
װאָס איז יוצא פֿאַר זיך
מיט אַן אָמן אין כאָר פֿון אונטערגאַנג.

*A veytik tsutsukukn vi fun yidishkayt*
*iz gevorn nisht mer vi khazones,*
*un oysgetriknt iz der kval*
*fun gantsn likhtikn ritual.*
*Zol fun yidishkayt vern*
*bloyz a folks-lid,*
*vos git a khap baym hartsn*
*un gist on mit varemn honik*
*fun dermonung di gederim?*
*Libersht nem aza yom tov un farshter im.*
*Du, yidisher dikhter, vos bist gevorn di bin,*
*un shtelst tsu dem honik-margarin,*
*vos is meytse mit gezang.*
*Nisht mer vi a meshoyrer bistu,*
*vos iz yoytse far zikh*
*mit an omeyn in khor fun untergang.*

**44**

It's agony to see that Jewishness
has become a cantor's call,
and dried up is the well
of the whole glowing ritual.
Shall Jewishness become
only a folk-song,
that catches at the heart
and coats the entrails
with the warm honey of memory?
Better to break up such a celebration.
You, Jewish poet, who have become the bee
and produce the honey margarine
that smears a slice of bread with song —
you are no more than a chorister
who has only enough
for an amen in the chorus of decline.

מיר האָבן זיך צופיל פאַרלאָזט אויפן זיכרון,
ביז ס'האָט טראָפּנוווייז פון אונדז
אַלץ אויסגעדענקט.
איצט זיינען מיר פאַרבענקט
נאָך אַ זמרל, נאָך אַ גראַם,
נאָך אַן אויסגעוועפטן טעם.
אַרום אונדזערע קעפּ דרייען מיר אַלע
אַ כּפרה-האָן,
אָבער דער געפּרעפּלטער תּיקון
גייט אונדז מער נישט אָן.
בענקשאַפט-יידישקייט איז אַ וויג-ליד פאַר זקנים,
וואָס טשקאַיען איינגעוווייקטע חלה.
זאָלן מיר צושטעלן די ווייכע קרישקעס,
די ווערטער אויסגעלעבטע און הוילע,
מיר וואָס האָבן געחלומט
פון אַ נייער אנשי כּנסת הגדולה?

Mir hobn zikh tsufil farlozt oyfn zikorn,
biz s'hot tropnvayz fun undz
alts oysgedenkt.
Itst zaynen mir farbenkt
nokh a zemerl, nokh a gram,
nokh an oysgeveptn tam.
Arum undzere kep dreyen mir ale
a kapore-hon,
ober der gepreplter tikun
geyt undz mer nisht on.
Benkshaft-yidishkayt iz a vig-lid far zekeynim,
vos tshkayen ayngeveykte khale.
Zoln mir tsushteln di veykhe krishkes,
di verter oysgelebte un hoyle,
mir vos hobn gekholemt
fun a nayer anshi kneses hagdoylu?

**44**

We relied too much on memory,
until drop by drop
all has been contrived out of us.
Now we are lonely
for a tune, a rhyme,
for an escaped flavor.
We all swing around our heads
the sacrificial hen.
But the murmured prayer's meaning
no longer interests us.
Nostalgia Jewishness is a lullaby for old men
gumming soaked white bread.
Shall we produce the soft crumbs,
the words lifeless and hollow,
we who had dreamed
of a new assembly of Men of the Great Temple?

דער ייד (פֿון "למד-וו")

איך בין שמואל-איצע קוימענקערער,
אַן אביון אַ פֿארהונגערטער פֿון רייסן,
איך האָב געליטן שטומערהייט און כ'קאָן ניט מערער,
און כ'קאָן ניט מערער לעבן אויף צופֿלייסן.

איך בין אויף וויסטע בוידימער געקראָכן
און קוימענס לאַנגע, פֿינצטערע געקערט,
איך האָב אויף קאַלטע דעכער אָפּגעלעבט די וואָכן,
און נאָר שבתים אָפּגעריכט אויף דר'ערד.

# DER YID

(Fun "Lamed Vov")

Ikh bin Shmuel-Itse koymenkerer,
an evyen a farhungerter fun raysn,
ikh hob gelitn shtumerheyt un kh'kon nit merer,
un kh'kon nit merer lebn oyf tsuflaysn.

Ikh bin oyf viste boydemer gekrokhn
un koymens lange, fintstere gekert,
ikh hob oyf kalte dekher opgelebt di vokhn,
un nor shabosim opgerikht oyf dr'erd.

# 45

# MOYSHE KULBAK

## THE JEW

(From "The Secret Saint")

I am Shmuel-Itse Chimneysweep,
starved from scrambling, a poor man.
I have suffered silently and can no more.
I can no longer live without a plan.

In dreary attics I have crawled
and tall and blackened chimneys swept;
on freezing roofs I lived out my weeks
and only Sabbaths on the ground I kept.

איך בין שבתים נאָר געגאַנגען אויף דער ערד,
אויף גרויע גאַסן, שלאָפעדיקע, צווישן קראָמען,
אויף שטילע מערק שפּאַצירנדיק האָב איך דערהערט
די שטים פון טיפע ברונימער און תהומען.
אָ, גאָט, פון ברונימער, פון פינצטערניש און תהומען!
פון טויזנט קוימענס האָב איך אַש אַרויסגענומען,
פאַרוואָס קאָן איך ניט אויסשעפּן דעם פּיין, וואָס האָט קיין נאָמען,
פאַרוואָס קאָן איך דעם אַש פון האַרצן ניט אַרויסבאַקומען?

. . . . . . . . . .

איך בין אַ ייד שמואל-איצע קוימענקערער,
ליג טיף אין קוימען פון דער וועלט און כ'שריי,
איך האָב געליטן שטומערהייט און כ'קאָן ניט מערער,
כאָטש ליידן וועל איך ווייטער סיי-ווי-סיי . . .

*Ikh bin shabosim nor gegangen oyf der erd,*
*oyf groye gasn, shlofedike, tsvishn kromen,*
*oyf shtile merk shpatsirndik hob ikh derhert*
*di shtim fun tife brunimer un tehomen.*
*O, got, fun brunimer, fun finsternish un tehomen!*
*Fun toyznt koymens hob ikh ash aroysgenumen,*
*farvos kon ikh nit oysshepn dem payn, vos hot kayn nomen,*
*farvos kon ikh dem ash fun hartsn nit aroysbakumen?*

. . . . . . . . . .

*Ikh bin a yid Shmuel-Itse koymenkerer,*
*lig tif in koymen fun der velt un kh'shray,*
*ikh hob gelitn shtumerheyt un kh'kon nit merer,*
*khotsh laydn vel ikh vayter say-vi-say . . .*

**45**

Only on Sabbaths I walked the earth,
among shops, on grey sleeping streets.
Strolling through still markets I heard
the voice of deep wells and profundities.
O God of wells, of darkness and of depth!
I have removed ashes from a thousand chimneys.
Why can't I drain off the grief, that has no name,
why, from my own heart, can't the ash be swept?

. . . . . . . . . . . . . . . . . .

I am the Jew Shmuel-Itse Chimneysweep,
lie deep in the chimneys of the world and I say:
I have suffered silently and I can no more,
although I'll go on suffering anyway.

מיינע "פֿאָטערלענדער"

פֿאָטערלענדער מיינע,
ווער קען אייך אויסצײלן און דאַכטן?
סיידן ציטעריקע פֿיס, וואָס פֿילן,
אַז שטרעקעס ליגן אייביקע און ווארטן.

ווארטן,
ווי אַ לייב אויף לויער,
ווארטן —
זיכערע געדולדיק,
אַז פֿיס זאָלן אָנקומען אין טרויער,
פֿיס —
וואָס זיינען אייביק שולדיק.

שרפֿות —
ווארטן, אַז מיר זאָלן צו זיי קומען,
אין שרפֿה האָט זיך גאָט צו אונדז געמאָלדן.


## MAYNE "FOTERLENDER"

Foterlender mayne,
ver ken aykh oystseyln un dakhtn?
Saydn tsiterike fis, vos filn,
az shtrekes lign eybike un vartn.

Vartn,
vi a leyb, oyf loyer,
vartn —
zikhere geduldik,
az fis zoln onkumen in troyer,
fis —
vos zaynen eybik shuldik.

Sreyfes —
vartn, az mir zoln tsu zey kumen,
in sreyfe hot zikh got tsu undz gemoldn.

# KADIE MOLODOWSKY

## MY "FATHERLANDS"

My fatherlands,
who can count or mention all of you,
except trembling feet that feel
distances lying eternally in wait?

Wait,
like a lion for its prey,
wait —
sure, patiently,
for feet to come in sad dismay,
feet —
that are forever guilty.

Fires —
await our approach;
in fire God has appeared to us.

ימים —

װארטן, אז מיר זאלן אין זיי זינקען,
מיר האבן איינמאל שוין דעם ים געשפאלטן.


פאטערלענדער מיינע,
קאלטע, הײסע, זוניקע און טריבע,
איך קאן אײך צוזאגן צו אקערן, צו זײען, צו באזינגען,
נאר כ'קען ניט צוזאגן קײן ליבע.


איך בין פארליבט גאר אין א קארשן־בײמל,
װאס האט געבליט, מיר דוכט זיך, אין א טאג א העלן,
איך בין געגאנגען אין א װײסן קלײדל
מיט א קרענצל גלעזערנע קארעלן.


פאטערלענדער מיינע,
הײסע, קאלטע, זוניקע און טריבע,
לאמיר רעדן װעגן גאט, און ברויט, און װאסער,
נאר לאמיר מער ניט רעדן װעגן ליבע.


*Yamen —*
*vartn, az mir zoln in zey zinken,*
*mir hobn eynmol shoyn dem yam geshpoltn.*

*Foterlender mayne,*
*kalte, heyse, zunike un tribe,*
*ikh kon aykh tsuzogn tsu akern, tsu zeyen, tsu bazingen,*
*nor kh'ken nit tsuzogn kayn libe.*

*Ikh bin farlibt gor in a karshn-beyml,*
*vos hot geblit, mir dukht zikh, in a tog a heln,*
*ikh bin gegangen in a vaysn kleydl*
*mit a krentsl glezerne kareln.*

*Foterlender mayne,*
*heyse, kalte, zunike un tribe,*
*lomir redn vegn got, un broyt, un vaser,*
*nor lomir mer nit redn vegn libe.*

**46**

Waters —
await our drowning;
we have once already split the sea.

My fatherlands,
cold, hot, full of sun or mud,
I can promise to plow you, sow you, sing of you,
but I cannot promise you my love.

My love is given to a cherry tree
that bloomed, it seems to me, on a day of light;
I was wearing a string of glass beads
upon a dress of white.

My fatherlands,
hot, cold, full of sun or mud,
let us talk of God, and bread, and water,
but let us talk no more of love.

# BIOGRAPHICAL NOTES

### Adler, Jacob   1877–

Born in Dinov, Galicia

He emigrated to America in 1894 and in 1907 published his first book of lyric poetry, *Zikhroynes*. Since then he has been known chiefly for his humorous verse, and after the death of Moyshe Nadir has been considered the dean of Yiddish humorous writers. He is a contributor to the Yiddish dailies and now lives in Florida.

### Almi, A. (A. H. Sheps)   1892–

Born in Warsaw, Poland

His first poems appeared when he was fifteen. He settled in America in 1913 and lives in New York. He is one of the more respected Yiddish essayists and critics and publishes regularly in the Yiddish press.

### Auerbach, Ephraim   1892–

Born in Belts, Bessarabia

In 1913 he became an agricultural laborer in what was then Palestine. When he was expelled by the Turks upon their entrance into World War I, he joined the Zion Mule Corps of the British Army in Alexandria and fought at the Dardanelles. In 1915 he was invalided out of the army and came to America, where he has since lived in New York. His first collection of poetry was *Karavanen* (New York, 1918), and he has continued to write regularly.

### Einhorn, David   1886–

Born in Korelitsh, Poland (White Russia)

The son of an army physician. At first he wrote poetry only in Hebrew, but after joining the Socialist Bund he began writing in Yiddish. His poetry alternates between love and nature lyrics, and proletarian verse. He has been much influenced by the Russian poet Alexander Blok. In 1912 he was exiled and lived in Switzerland, Berlin, and Paris. He first visited America in 1925 and now lives in New York, where he writes for the newspapers and periodicals.

## Glatstein, Jacob (Gladstone)   1896–

Born in Lublin, Poland

In 1914 he settled in America, where he studied law. He wrote poetry at the age of seventeen, but not until 1919 did he focus his energies on Yiddish literature. He was one of the founders of the *In Zikh* group and writes a regular column for a Yiddish daily newspaper. His prize-winning novel is *Ven Yash Iz Geforn,* and he is an excellent critic and commentator on the political and literary scene.

## Grade, Chaim   1910–

Born in Vilna, Poland

After his father, a night-watchman, died, Grade lived in a children's home. He was educated in the traditional Yeshiva and belonged to the *Yung Vilna* group of artists founded in 1929. He fled to Russia when Vilna was taken by the Nazis and has now come to live in New York.

## Halpern, Moyshe Leyb   1886–1933

Born in Zlotshev, East Galicia

He received a scant education in Hebrew as well as in other languages. At the age of twelve he went to Vienna to learn to be a sign painter. For ten years he lived among Christians and became a good swimmer and football player. He was influenced by Nietzsche, Lilienkron, and Richard Dehmel, and his first poetry was written in German. After his return home he was guided by the older Galician Yiddish poets and wrote in Yiddish. In 1908 he came to America to escape military service. He was a member of the *Yunge,* edited newspapers and magazines in New York, and was a good graphic artist.

## Iceland, Reuben (Eisland)   1884–1953

Born in Great-Radomishl, Galicia

He came to America in 1903, where he joined the *Yunge.* He was at first a factory worker. His collected works, *Fun Mayn Zumer,* appeared in 1922. He has translated Chinese and German literature (most of Heine's work) into English. He lived and published in New York.

# Kulbak, Moyshe    1896–1937?

Born in Smargon, in the district of Vilna, Russian Poland

His father was a forest worker, his mother the daughter of a peasant family. Although his parents were very devout, they sent him, as a child, to a Yiddish folk-school. Later he attended the regular orthodox Jewish schools and was a Yeshiva student until he was eighteen. His reading background was very broad, in Hebrew, Yiddish, and Russian, and his first poems were written in Hebrew. He later wrote only in Yiddish. At the outbreak of World War I he was a teacher of Hebrew in Kovno. His first published poem, "Shterndl," 1916, was sung, almost at once, as a folk song. In 1920 he went to Berlin to study; and his experience there he has recorded in a long narrative poem, "Disner Childe Harold." He wrote plays in addition to the poetry and short novels he had been regularly publishing and translated German poetry into Yiddish. In 1923 he returned to Vilna to become a teacher in the Yiddish schools and devoted himself to new interests: public speaking and writing essays, as well as continuing his other writing. In 1928 he moved to the Soviet Union, drawn by politics and by his trouble in establishing Polish citizenship and because he wanted to be near his family in Minsk. By 1931 he had written a remarkable novel of Jewish life in Russia since the Revolution: he did not glorify the "new" generation but rather the old. When the second volume was published in 1935, there was evidence of his attempts to make his story more palatable by Soviet standards. In 1937 the Yiddish State Theater of Moscow produced his folk comedy, *Boytre,* but despite (or perhaps because of) the critical acclaim it received, a representative of the police appeared at the second performance and announced its closing — the author had been arrested. Rumors placed him in a concentration camp in the Orel district, and his death may have occurred in the early forties. I have given his biography in detail for its classic implications.

# Landau, Zisha    1889–1937

Born in Plotsk, Poland

A descendant of famous rabbis, he received a traditional orthodox education. His Hebrew teacher taught him to love Heine, by whose works he was influenced. In 1906 he settled in New York, where he was one of the founders and leaders of the *Yunge.*

## Leib, Mani (Mani Leib Brahinsky) 1883–1953

Born in Niezshen, Russian Poland

He received a traditional Jewish education until the age of thirteen, when he was apprenticed to a shoemaker. He became a successful business man and then a revolutionist. In 1904 he was imprisoned for revolutionary activities and upon his second arrest he ran away to England. He settled in America in 1905, where he published over two thousand poems and translations. His early poetic idols were Pushkin and Lermontov.

## Leivick, H. (Halper) 1888–

Born in Yihumen, White Russia

At the age of sixteen he was expelled from the Yeshiva for reading anti-religious books. From 1906 to 1910 he was in the Moscow jail for membership in the Socialist Bund. He was exiled to Siberia for life in 1912, but in 1913 escaped to New York. He earned his living as a house-painter and decorator, and later spent years in tuberculosis sanatoria. He has earned a reputation as a writer of verse drama and is among the most highly regarded of the contemporary Yiddish poets.

## Manger, Itzik 1901–

Born in Czernowitz, Bukovina

He attended a German Evangelical school until the age of twelve and lived for a while in Berlin. He wrote German poetry and was influenced by Rainer Maria Rilke. In 1918 he began writing in Yiddish and has become one of the very best Yiddish poets of our day. He has experimented with poetry in archaic Yiddish and has also written critical essays. Many of his poems have been set to music and are sung as folk songs. Upon his escape from Europe, he lived for a while in London and now lives in New York.

## Molodowsky, Kadie 1893–

Born in Lithuania

She made her literary debut in 1920 and was a teacher in Warsaw and worked on left-wing newspapers. In 1936 she came to America after persecution by the Fascist Polish political police, following the publication of her *Dzhike Gas*. Her poetry since then shows the influence of the American scene, and of Israel, where she paid long visits. She lives in New York.

## Ravitch, Melech (Zachariah-Khane Bergner)   1893–

Born in Radimno, East Galicia

He received no formal religious or worldly education but was trained for his father's business. In Lemburg he came into contact with the Galician Yiddish writers (Halpern among them) and in 1902 published his first poem. In 1913 he settled in Vienna and was an Austrian soldier for a short while during World War I. In 1921 he moved to Warsaw where he edited many periodicals and newspapers. He has traveled extensively and is presently in Israel, after having lived and worked in South America, Mexico, Montreal, Australia, and New York.

## Sutskever, Abraham   1913–

Born in Smargon

In 1915 the Cossacks burned Smargon and the family wandered to Omsk in Siberia. His father, a rabbi, died there, and the family moved to Vilna. In Vilna, Sutskever received his education and, under the influence of Halpern, Leivick, and Kulbak, joined the *Yung Vilna* group and in 1933 published his first poetry. When the Nazis entered Vilna he escaped, saving many valuable archives from the Jewish museum of which he was then curator. He became a member of a Partisan corps and later joined the Russian army. When Russia freed Vilna he returned there. His published accounts (translated in the American newspapers in 1944) of the Vilna massacres are among the few eye-witness reports of Nazi activities recorded by an artist. He is now living in Israel.

## Zeitlin, Aaron   1889–

Born in White Russia

The son of Hillel Zeitlin, a noted Yiddish writer. He lived in Vilna and after 1907 in Warsaw. He visited Palestine and America in 1920 and settled in New York before the beginning of World War II. He has published poetry and essays in both Yiddish and Hebrew and is among the most erudite of the Yiddish poets.